The Author

Create your dream career and lifestyle, writing and self-publishing non-fiction books

FIONA FERRIS

Copyright © 2020 Fiona Ferris
All rights reserved.

ISBN: 9798647207517

Other books by Fiona Ferris

Thirty Chic Days: *Practical inspiration for a beautiful life*

Thirty More Chic Days: *Creating an inspired mindset for a magical life*

Thirty Chic Days Vol. 3: *Nurturing a happy relationship, staying youthful, being your best self, and having a ton of fun at the same time*

Thirty Slim Days: *Create your slender and healthy life in a fun and enjoyable way*

Financially Chic: *Live a luxurious life on a budget, learn to love managing money, and grow your wealth*

How to be Chic in the Winter: *Living slim, happy and stylish during the cold season*

How to be Chic in the Summer: *Living well, keeping your cool and dressing stylishly when it's warm outside*

A Chic and Simple Christmas: *Celebrate the holiday season with ease and grace*

The Original 30 Chic Days Blog Series: *Be inspired by the online series that started it all*

30 Chic Days at Home: *Self-care tips for when you have to stay at home, or any other time when life is challenging*

The Chic Closet: *Inspired ideas to develop your personal style, fall in love with your wardrobe, and bring back the joy in dressing yourself*

The Peaceful Life: *Slowing down, choosing happiness, nurturing your feminine self, and finding sanctuary in your home*

Loving Your Epic Small Life: *Thriving in your own style, being happy at home, and the art of exquisite self-care*

The Glam Life: *Uplevel everything in a fun way using glamour as your filter to the world*

100 Ways *to Live a Luxurious Life on a Budget*

100 Ways *to Declutter Your Home*

100 Ways *to Live a European Inspired Life*

Contents

Introduction 9

Chapter 1 *How I became a successful author in a few short years* 14

Chapter 2 *What to write about?* 20

Chapter 3 *Don't settle for a mediocre life!* 29

Chapter 4 *How to find the time to write* 36

Chapter 5 *Create a motivating goal for yourself* .. 44

Chapter 6 *My favourite way to structure my writing* 51

Chapter 7   *How to write* 60

Chapter 8   *How would SHE show up?* 69

Chapter 9   *How to get past your fears* 78

Chapter 10   *Write fast* 85

Chapter 11   *The flow of your book and 'extras'* 94

Chapter 12   *The hidden benefits of exploring your author fantasy* 108

Chapter 13   *How to edit your book* 114

Chapter 14   *Creating a beautiful cover for your book* 129

Chapter 15   *Formatting your book for publication* 139

Chapter 16   *Self-publishing or traditional publishing?* 154

Chapter 17   *Why I chose Amazon to publish my books* 164

Chapter 18   *Pricing your book for success* 172

Chapter 19 *How to market your book for free* 181

Chapter 20 *How to gain readership for your blog and social media pages* 197

Chapter 21 *Just start!* 205

100 Ways to Create Your Dream Life as a Successful Author 211

A Note from the Author 235

About the Author 237

Introduction

Welcome, author-to-be! I know you dream of being a writer, of being able to hold in your hands a book with your name on the cover. I know you have a manuscript inside you that you want to tell others about, even if you don't *quite* know what it will say yet.

Perhaps you dream of beautifying the world with your words, maybe even being able to quit your job in doing so. Imagine how that would feel, earning your own income by becoming part of your most favourite world – the world of books, words, authors, eBooks, and publishing.

I know it sounds scary. It's a professional thing that surely you can't be a part of, right? But guess what, times have changed. No longer do you have to wait for permission from someone else to be a published author. I'll tell you the secret, right here in the introduction and you can start creating your dream life as an author today. All you have to do is **write about what most makes you happy, and upload it**. That's all! There are a few other bits and pieces to it, but at its most simple, that's all you have to do.

If you're anything like me though, you've overcomplicated things in the past and it's probably ended up with you getting nowhere. You have the thought of, 'I *know* I could write a book, and it would be fabulous. People would love it.' Then your mind immediately starts backpedalling, 'Whaaat! No way, don't be ridiculous.'

I know this because I had the same thoughts circling around in my head for a long time. That's why it took me a full year to finish my first book *Thirty Chic Days* (and it was already half-written before that), but only three months each, give or take, for my later books. I found out what is vitally important and what is not necessary. I found the shortcuts I could take, as well as getting my successful author mindset in place (the most important thing!)

I look forward to sharing all my success tips in the coming chapters: tried and proven steps I took that helped me publish my books, earn money from them and create a beautiful work-from-home lifestyle that has enriched my life.

So, if this sounds fun and exciting to you, welcome. I hope you have a little tingle of excitement in your stomach for *your* future success. It's totally doable!

This book is for you if you:

- have a life-long dream of writing a book but think it will never happen.

- love reading and wonder if there might be a book inside you, but have no clue how to go about it.

- would love to be an author but don't know where to start, and whether you'd be any good at it.

- have information to share with others.

- want to start a new career.

- have already written or even published a book but are looking for extra inspiration and a few new success strategies. (I love reading about how other authors structure their writing, plan their day and motivate themselves!)

Basically, if you have any interest at all in writing or being an author, you will get a lot from this book. I am here to tell you that you *can* create something just from your own ideas and hard work. You can make a living doing something you love. Yes, it will be 'work', but I promise you it is worth the effort.

My goal for this book is that you will transform a vague yearning to write into a roadmap, clearly lit and full of signs, ready to help you to embark on your author career.

You can be assured that this book has been written by a very real and approachable person (me!) who has had success in self-publishing, yet knows the fears, challenges and realities of putting your own work out there.

Another benefit is the (very gentle) kick in the pants from me to you to start writing. Perhaps you have wanted to be an author, but never felt ready. Perhaps you have been 'getting ready' for years now, but never even written a single word.

I hear that voice in your heart... where your dreams live, to be a writer. I want you to feel hugged, supported, encouraged... and have you believe that you can do this. Not only believe, but be champing at the bit to get started.

Or perhaps you are someone who has never lacked in ideas, but often felt that you were "floundering" when attempting to begin writing, and maintain a consistent schedule. In these pages you will gain the inspiration, knowledge and confidence to help you go after your dreams.

If writing has always been something you have been drawn to and curious about, but has seemed overwhelming to you, you will be happy to know that my motivational style is accessible, warm and welcoming. My personal way is to be fun, kind, non-judgemental, and I have a get-things-done attitude without drama.

I know myself that being a published author is an amazing experience and I would be honoured to be your writing mentor if you choose to follow the chapters in this book and make your writing dreams come true.

Let's go!

Fiona

Chapter 1
How I became a successful author in a few short years

I am often asked if I have been an author for a long time because I have several books out. It has been five years that I have been writing and releasing my books, which I guess is a decent amount of time, but quite short too considering how long I dreamed of being an author for.

I have always been a big reader though, right from an early age, and always had in my mind the thought of writing a book 'one day'. But how? Getting an agent or manager sounded so difficult. Where did you find one? What was the difference between the two? And which did you need first?

Then I got realistic: I live in New Zealand, a tiny country at the bottom of the world with a population less than five million people. I told myself it would be okay if I lived in the United States where there was much more of an audience, but just how many books could I possibly sell in New Zealand?

It seemed an impossible dream which I didn't really consider seriously, just took out of its box every now and then to sigh at and put away again.

Then... the Internet happened. And blogs. And the new wave of self-publishing opportunities on offer.

In 2004 I came across a blog and it spoke to me. The author lived in America and wrote about regaining her femininity after having her first child. Her posts were so pretty and inspiring that I was hooked. About four years after that I began a blog of my own and started creating my own inspiration.

Facebook and Twitter had only just started, and Instagram hadn't even been invented yet. It sounds so long ago, but it wasn't really.

I started seeing bloggers publish their own books, but again, it took me a while to try this for myself. Eventually in 2015 I published a series of three short eBooks to both test the waters and also work out how this self-publishing thing worked. The eBooks were compilations of favourite posts from my blog *How to be Chic*, and from day one people ordered them.

This gave me the confidence to carry on with the half-written book which sat in my desk drawer at home. Approximately every six months I'd come across it (a bundle of printed-out computer pages) and start reading. It wasn't half-bad! Inspired, I would write another chapter. Then, beset with self-doubt, I'd add the new pages and put it back into the drawer again.

That book was *Thirty Chic Days*. I outlined it years previous, but it had a lot of false starts. If I knew then what I know now, I would have finished it much quicker, but I am a believer in perfect timing so how it happened was how it was meant to happen.

When my writing really got going and I started earning a monthly income from it, I had the thrilling thought that I could cut my hours down to part-time, and spend more time at home being a happy housewife and writer. I am a home-loving introvert who is happiest in her own company and her own little dream world. My ultimate wish was not to go to a job at all, but to be at home full-time, with my laptop and pets, writing my books.

Well, it happened. My income surpassed what I could earn in a full-time job, let alone a part-time job. My dream life had come true and it continues to this day.

I still pinch myself that this is my reality. I am a self-employed, fully supported writer and have been for three years now. I truly believe that if I can do it, anyone with a desire to write can do it.

I don't have any formal training, but what I do have is a love for reading and writing, and a desire to share my favourite ideas and inspiration with my readers. I also have the self-confidence that I am going to write my books whether anyone reads them or not. I really am writing my books for me now, and I probably couldn't stop; I love doing it so much.

I am also grateful to current technology which means I can upload a book to Kindle and have readers download it soon after. I can format my own print book and have readers order copies which are printed on demand and sent out to them a day or two later. How mind-bogglingly awesome is that?

And I am especially grateful to all the lovely readers who have read my books and written amazing reviews and sent me happy emails. I have had only one not-so-nice email and yes, I do have some one- and two-star reviews on Amazon, but I don't let those upset me because I can't be everyone's cup of tea.

I give my very best to each book and sure, I would love everyone to love my writing, but I know it's just not possible. We all have different tastes in what we find enjoyable. (Even the most popular writers receive their share of one-star reviews.) Yes, writing has taught me a lot, including humbleness.

It has also taught me the satisfaction of seeing my books published and of hearing my late dad say how proud he was of me.

And crazy things can happen too, such as emails arriving from publishing houses in foreign countries asking if they can translate my books. Yes, that has happened to me, three times so far, and I now have books published in Lithuanian and Russian with Vietnamese coming soon.

It just goes to show what you can set in motion when you follow your dreams.

Your desire is reality waiting in the wings

If you have always wanted to write a book, know that that desire is within you for a reason, and if you have that dream, *it is possible*. You are never given the desire for something without it being available to you.

It doesn't matter how many trazillion books there are published already, *there is room for yours*. No matter how niche your topic might be, you will find your readers. I implore you not to keep pushing down that dream of publishing your book. It feels incredible, and I want my enthusiasm, motivation and self-belief to be contagious to you.

Just for a minute, imagine seeing yourself in a year's time – or even sooner – having published your first book and starting on your second. Imagine seeing happy reviews of your book online. Imagine logging into your online banking and seeing royalty payments that have been deposited overnight. Imagine receiving emails from foreign publishing houses wanting to translate your books.

Don't listen to the naysayers and those who say you can't make a living from writing. The only people you want to listen to are *those who are doing what you want to do.* So, listen to me, and others like me. Listen to those who are making things happen, not those who are sitting at home on the sofa complaining that nothing interesting ever works out for them.

You have to make your own luck in life, and I promise you, it's not that hard and it's so worth it! I can't wait for you to read the rest of this book, write your book, and tell me what it's called so I can go and order it. Exciting times!

Chapter 2
What to write about?

When I was dreaming of being an author I always thought I would write fiction books. But when I started my blog and could write about whatever I wanted to, I didn't start a fictional serialized story. I wrote about living a chic French-inspired life without spending a lot of money, and without moving to Paris.

Writing my posts never felt like I was forcing anything because I loved this topic. I loved to daydream about my perfect rose-tinted lifestyle and how I could bring elegance and sophistication to my normal everyday life here in New Zealand.

Thanks to my blog, I had a clear vision in my head for what my books would *feel* like before I had even written a single word of my first book. But, please be reassured that you don't need to have an online presence already though. In this chapter I will share with you all my tips and secrets on finding out what to write about.

Perhaps you are one of the lucky ones who knows exactly what you want to cover. Perhaps you have a vague idea or perhaps you want to be a writer – badly – yet have no clue what you want to speak to the world about.

There is all sorts of good advice around such as 'write about what you love' or 'write what you know' and I'd agree with them. But they're a bit... wishy washy, don't you think? Some of us need more guidance, something more concrete to work with. Something to inspire great action!

Write about what you love

To start with, the best and easiest way to distill your thoughts down into an actionable list of book topic possibilities is just that – have a fun brainstorming session where you list everything you love to read about, study, talk on and work with.

You choose your flavour of what you are going to do - What do you love doing and what do you not? Strengths and weaknesses? - What are you naturally good at? What do you do for fun? - What makes you feel happy and excited?

Depending on how your mind works best, you could make lists (my favourite way), draw mind maps with coloured pens, or create mood boards on Pinterest or by cutting out images and words from magazine pages.

Another great way to see what you are drawn to is to look at your bookshelf or Kindle content. What themes are there? What are your favourite books about? This list is great not only to pinpoint what topics interest you the most, but you can also note down book ideas. I have often thought to myself, 'I'd love to do my own version of this (book or topic)' and so it goes down on my book ideas list.

You might start out with separate lists doing these kinds of exercises, but you will quickly realize that all the topics start looking similar, and even if not, you may see that they mesh together nicely to provide a symbiotic feeling. Marry together the different sides of yourself and see what it looks like.

For me, I love to study and write about:

- Living well on little money

- Living a chic and French-inspired lifestyle

- Curating the perfect capsule wardrobe

- Having a simple, peaceful and serene life

- Being a good steward of my money

- Personal development, levelling up and self-improvement

- Having an orderly, streamlined and decluttered home

In my world these all come under the umbrella of living a chic and beautiful lifestyle without spending a lot of money, but rather by cultivating an elegance mindset. And that's what I write about.

What you love is nobody else's business

I have always enjoyed these topics but learned not to talk to others about them unless I could sense that they were like me, because I was made fun of a few times which hurt! That's when I realized it is better not to talk so much about my rich inner world and instead let it fuel me from the inside. And, write my books about it.

You don't need to listen to other people when they try to give you advice on what to write about. What you love, you love. If they want to write a book, they can.

When someone gives me their unsolicited advice, I simply smile, nod my head and thank them, then do exactly what I was going to anyway. And, from these experiences I have vowed never to give unsolicited advice again!

Each of us has our own topics which most excite us, whether we write books or not. As you know from listening to other people, it's sometimes hard to see what makes them so passionate about their hobbies and interests, because they're not *your* hobbies and interests.

That's why it is so important to stay true to what *you* love. If you chose to write a book on a topic that didn't particularly interest you very much, it would be hard going. It can be tough enough completing a book even when you love the topic, so give yourself the best chance of success by choosing topics that make your heart go pitter-pat.

Write what you know

Another great way to come up with possible book ideas is to list everything you can think of that you have experienced in life. You might have thrived after divorce, looked after a sick child or elderly parent, conquered a serious illness, climbed a mountain, or gained a degree or new job against the odds.

In one of my books – *Financially Chic* – I talk about how my husband and I bought our first home and paid it off within five years. In my mind that's quite an unusual achievement and one that I am proud of. I'm sure that others would also be interested in reading how we did that.

What have you done that you want to share the nuts and bolts of with others? What could you inspire, educate or enlighten readers with? Have you home-schooled children, slashed your grocery budget in half with batch cooking or created a home-based business from nothing?

There literally is a market for every kind of book these days, which is exciting for us both as writers and readers. I'm sure as much time as I spend writing my own books, I spend just as much time browsing for, purchasing and reading self-published Kindle books by other authors.

What if you don't have a clear vision?

Some of us are multi-passionate; I know I am. I don't want to stick with just one topic and would rather write on many different topics. But as you can see from my examples earlier in this chapter, they are fairly cohesive. Perhaps when you look at yours, you will find they link as well.

But if this doesn't apply to you, please don't let not knowing what to write about stop you from writing (how's that for a mind-twisty sentence). If you have many ideas and passions, why not start with the first one that comes to mind and let your topics choose themselves?

Just start writing a chapter and see where it goes. Think of it as a task you've been set: 'Write a 1,500-word essay on the topic of your choice'. Maybe it's what you want people to know about. Maybe it's advice to your younger self. Maybe it's what is top of mind for you today.

Brainstorming book ideas

I find it easier to write when I have a big, beautiful list of ideas to choose from. It's like being at the most fun buffet ever. Before I even do that though, I find it helpful to brainstorm *topic-finding questions*. Here are a few of my favourites:

1. What is a problem area that you could work through in a book which would then help others?

2. What are ten topics you absolutely adore reading about?

3. What is that one area in your life where you feel you have really 'nailed it'?

4. If you have a blog or social media account, what do you post about?

5. What topics are you passionate, almost obsessive, about?

6. What are books you have been inspired by that you could do your own 'take' or version of?

7. What do you find it easy to do in life? Something that others compliment you on that you think, 'Surely everyone knows how to do that?'

8. What is your WOW factor? What makes you different from other people?

9. What clubs or organizations do you belong to? List them down and see if they give you any clues for topics that light you up.

10. Take a favourite theme or hobby and brainstorm twenty topics within that theme.

11. If you have notebooks full of quotes and inspiration, browse through them and see what ideas and topics are represented over and over.

12. What are your top ten goals in life? Is one or more of them a topic you would love to write about?

You can choose one of these questions to brainstorm twenty answers to, or you can have a brainstorming session of your own to come up with *your* questions: try for twenty, thirty, fifty or even one-hundred questions. I regularly come up with ten or twenty, but it's when you get to the higher numbers that, while it's more difficult, you come up with some great ideas.

Successful author action tips:

Don't discount any ideas: write them all down. **Have an ideas notebook** where you capture thoughts that pop into your head; a sentence from a movie that you think, 'that is a great title for a book'; and books or online posts by others that you want to explore for your own version of. An example of book titles that might inspire me are: *My Year of Decluttering* or *I Decluttered My Whole Life*. Something in me is sparked off and I start thinking, 'What a fun project. And I could write about it too!'

It doesn't matter that something might have been written about hundreds or even thousands of times before – **your book won't be like any of those** because it comes from your perspective. I've often thought that if you gave one hundred people the same book title, chapter headings and sub-headings to write a book with, you would get a hundred different books.

And that's why I love to read books in the 'French Chic' genre by different authors, because they all bring something new to the table. And so it is for you – you don't need to worry about other similar authors, because **there is no competition**. You can all write alongside each other, and readers will buy and enjoy multiple books on the same topic.

Chapter 3
Don't settle for a mediocre life!

I don't know about you, but I never wanted a 'normal' life. It sounded boring to me, but at the same time I knew I wasn't one of those people who would give away all their possessions and spend their life travelling the world. The alternative of sacrificing everything to build an empire and become a multi-zillionaire wasn't me either.

No, I love my safe and comfortable life where I spend tons of time at home, simply because I am a homebody and it makes me happy to be there.

I do know that I'm not like everyone else though. I have done something quite different by writing the kinds of books I love, and encouraging others to live their dream life also. Whether it's creating your own income by becoming a self-published author or deciding that you are going to live a romantic life filled with style and *joie de vivre* regardless of others around you; why not carry it out?

When it comes to being a chic success in life, no matter what that success looks like for you, most people can't be bothered. It's too much effort and they really aren't willing to do what it takes. It's far more fun to sit on the sofa every night, eating chocolate and watching television.

A small disclaimer here: I love sitting on the sofa eating chocolate and watching television, but it's not my main source of pleasure. My main source of pleasure is that I don't have to go to a job every day.

I get to write my books, keep in touch with readers through my blog and social media, walk the dogs, hang out laundry in between chapters, go grocery shopping at quiet times (when it's just me and all the retirees in the area) and put the kettle on if my husband calls and says he's driving past and is popping home for an Earl Grey tea.

I love having that flexibility. I also love that I don't have to choose between being a happy homemaker and earning an income.

Create your own luck, and lifestyle

People have said to me, 'Oh, you're so lucky!' and yes, I do feel extremely fortunate the way things have worked out, but I've also put the effort in to make it happen. I created a compelling vision for myself which pulled me along when I was just getting started.

Occasionally I'll come across an old notebook where I have written my top ten goals in every day, perhaps from years ago, and it's a huge thrill to see that many of my daydreams have come to fruition. My goals consistently said things like, 'I am so happy and grateful to write books from my beautiful home office. We live on a semi-rural property with our happy pets. Paul has a job that he loves and we both earn great money. Life is wonderful and we couldn't ask for anything more perfect for us!'

These notebook scribbles have now come true and I put it down to my early willingness to spend time writing about what made me happy, having the guts to put my work out there for public opinion, ignoring the self-doubt in my head (which still shows up to this day) and continue writing the next book, and the next.

These are hard things for a lot of people and I want to say to you now, don't let them be. Let them be easy. Let your words flow without judgement, and let yourself fill notebook after notebook with goals and ideas. Ideas of how you want your dream lifestyle as an author to look. Ideas for your book titles and content. Ideas of what you will look like in your new life. How you will dress as a successful author living your dream life (hint: it doesn't have to be fancy; I live a very casual life, but I still love to have a touch of elegance).

Be willing to change things up. A lot of people have told me they want to write a book, but very few of them actually have. Don't be that person who wishes and dreams, but never does. It takes determination, yes, and you may have to juggle things around to find the time. But it's *so worth it*. I can't say that enough.

Don't be 'the excuse girl'

I want to tell you a 'funny' story: I had a friend-of-a-friend email me years ago when I was still working full-time. She'd heard how well I was doing and wanted to ask how I had written my books and built my online following, because she wanted to do the same. I wrote to her and shared all the steps I'd taken and asked what she planned to write about.

She wrote back and told me just how busy she was and that she wanted to write a book but couldn't really fit it into her life – she provided me with a long list of reasons why she didn't have any time to write. I was quite dumbfounded and wondered why she sought me out for advice. Maybe she thought I had a magic answer that didn't actually involve her writing? Aren't people interesting! And also, in the time that she'd written her email full of excuses, I mean reasons, she could have written a chapter or outlined a book.

For me, it's not finding the time, it's finding the *motivation*. Because when I am inspired to do something it effortlessly comes ahead of other activities such as watching television or browsing the Internet. When I find myself lit up because of something I've read or listened to, I can't wait to get cracking on a project.

I know you are not that person who wishes and hopes she could be a writer, but can't really be bothered. You want to be different from others. You are not mediocre! You know that you want to write your book and break out of the hum-drum mould that most people are content to reside in.

And it's not like it takes *that much* effort either. If you decided you are going to dedicate an hour a day, or a four-hour block each week perhaps, to writing your book, you would be further ahead in three months than most people would be in three years.

The reason for this is that most people would rather *consume* than *create*, and I can find myself falling back into that trap even today. Sometimes I realize it's been a few days, a week or even longer that I haven't written anything and it's hard to get started again. Instead I've been consuming other people's information in the form of books – both fiction and non-fiction, podcasts, YouTube videos and television instead of actually creating my own stuff.

On the other hand, when I start off my day by choosing to write for thirty to sixty minutes, it provides momentum. I find it easier to write, and my mind pops out new ideas all the time.

Far from feeling deprived when I am up writing at 6am while most people are still snoozing, or doing a final read-through on a Saturday afternoon when others might be out shopping and coffee-ing, I feel amazing. I am creating assets for the future with my own mind, and it feels incredible.

I love being different to 99% of the population, because when you look at how most people live, they don't seem very inspired or happy with their lot. They are simply plodding through their days, self-medicating with food, drink, shopping and television until one day they'll die.

And then they complain that nothing exciting ever happens for them!

I know that sounds a bit rude and judgemental, but sometimes this is the kind of thinking that is required to be successful (don't get me wrong, I certainly love food, drink, shopping and television, but when I indulge too much at the expensive of creativity and motivation, it doesn't feel good). The key is to enjoy everything in its place *and* be a person who creates their own luck.

Successful author action tips:

Do you want to live a mediocre life, or would you rather live in a way that makes you feel **alive, excited, creative and abundant**?

Decide today that **you are a person who makes things happen**. Leave behind all thoughts of living an ordinary life and decide that yours is going to be **magical, wonderful, amazing and incredible**. Start with those thoughts in mind as you design the way you want your life to be.

Don't look to the normal person when you are creating your life; **look to the ones who are making successes of themselves** and doing great things (and by great things, I don't mean building skyscrapers; great things can be small things too, such as my dream to be a happy housewife who works from home.)

Take inspiration from others as you devise your own dream life. **Keep your eye on the prize** and don't be dragged down by negative talk or complainers. Have faith that the future will be amazing and do something towards that amazing future every single day.

Chapter 4
How to find the time to write

You might think it's impossible to start a new career, at the same time as working full-time and taking care of your responsibilities.

Now this is a big one when you're still working full-time and wanting to try something new. When I was learning to self-publish, I worked full-time in the business my husband Paul and I owned at the time. It was a retail footwear store, and for the most part we had no staff – it was just the two of us. In retail you really need to be open seven days, so between us we covered those seven days.

Paul worked six days and I worked five. We didn't have a day off together unless it was a public holiday where we weren't legally allowed to open, such as Easter or Christmas day. We worked many other public holidays and kept our eyes on the prize – we knew that by working those extra days we could put money onto our home mortgage and pay it off quicker.

But even though we worked a lot, we still saw each other most days at work, so it wasn't all bad. And we made sure evenings were our relaxing time. We very rarely took work home.

I would write at work sometimes, but I mostly wrote at home, simply because it was easier to keep in the zone without the door buzzer signalling a customer to break my train of thought.

I am a morning person, so I set my alarm one hour earlier than my usual wakeup time and used that hour to write. I was full of enthusiasm so it wasn't hard to do – I couldn't wait to get up and write each morning. I wrote chapter after chapter with a big mug of hot tea on my desk. I still love writing early with hot tea. In fact, Paul bought me a special giant mug for my writing desk, because I always went back for a second cup – what a sweetheart!

If you aren't a morning person, find that hour a day to write. You might come alive at night, so could settle in at 9pm after dinner's finished with and the children are in bed. I don't have kids, it didn't work out for Paul and I, so I know I have more time than most mums, but I still believe it can be done because I have seen other ladies do it.

Highly successful author Jennifer L. Scott of the *Madame Chic* series has four children and has just released her latest book. Plus she posts inspiring YouTube videos every week as well. I actually think she has a Superwoman cape on beneath her stylish 10-item wardrobe. Jennifer's example reminds me that if she can do it, so can I. And you can too.

Perhaps you have a long commute on public transport. Can you jot ideas down in a notebook instead of gazing out the window? Listen to inspiring audiobooks, or read motivational eBooks on your Kindle? Maybe you have an iPad or mini-laptop you can type on, and write a bit each day as you go to and from work.

If you drive to work, listen to inspiring audiobooks, podcasts or YouTube videos. I have listened to hundreds, if not thousands, of hours of motivating and mind-enriching information this way.

If you go out to a café for lunch each day, take your laptop or a spiral notebook with you and write for half an hour while you eat. I find that linking my writing time to other things means I'll do it. Yes, excitement for what you are doing will help, but making it routine and habitual will add that extra layer of 'cement'.

My writing-with-tea as soon as I get up is one example. Committing to writing 1,000 or 2,000 words, or one chapter, or for half an hour when you get home from work is another. Choose the measurement that works best for you and say you'll do it.

My measurement for this book is at least one chapter a day. I have decided that each chapter will be a minimum of 1,500 words and I have brainstormed a list of chapters, so I choose one topic first thing in the morning and aim to complete that chapter. Then I go for a walk, take a shower, eat breakfast and carry on with my other tasks for the day.

Enlist help from others if you need to

When we both worked full-time, Paul started cooking more at my request. We shared the meals turn-about during the week, whereas before that I did most of the weekday dinners. He could see I was serious about finishing my book, so he didn't mind. And I felt good about asking because I was determined to keep on going and publish that book.

If you have older children, can they have one night a week where they cook? My nieces are twelve and ten, and I see photos on my sister's Instagram account of evening meals they have helped produce. Even if the 'salad' is just chopped cucumber, which I saw on one dinner post!

There are also food delivery services which save you time and energy by dropping off dinner ingredients and recipes to your front door. I don't have a regular subscription but have used them every now and then.

And housework too... that's a big one. We decided we would both do housework, but on different days. On his day off Paul would do the vacuuming, mopping, bathrooms and toilets. On my day off I'd do laundry washing, drying and folding, as well as change the sheets on the bed. I'd mostly do grocery shopping as well.

One particularly busy December we asked the couple who cleaned our store to come weekly to our home and do the housework. It felt like *such* a huge and extravagant treat and I loved coming home to a clean house. I decided one day I would have that permanently.

Well, that's another of my dreams that has come true. We now have a cleaning team – two lovely ladies who come in once a week for an hour and do all the housework. I love it so much that I would give up other things in order to keep this service. I can happily write in my home office and not worry that the windowsills haven't been dusted in ages or the carpet needs vacuuming, because it's done every Thursday.

I feel good that I am supporting a small local business, and, there is another feelgood factor: one of the women I employ dreams of starting her own gourmet chutney and relish company, and is inspired by my self-created work-from-home lifestyle. She can see that she too could take her greatest passion and make a living from it.

If funds don't stretch to a cleaner or meal delivery service, there is still plenty you can do. When we were super-thrifty firstly on a low income, and then as we were motoring ahead on our mortgage, we simplified our home environment to cut down on housework, batch cooked so there would be extra meals in the freezer, and I deleted hobby spending (such as sewing and knitting supplies) committing to use up my stash of fabric and yarn – other craft-lovers will know what I am talking about.

I also stopped leisure shopping and replaced that with my writing and blogging. It was a win/win/win situation here: I saved money because I wasn't out mindlessly consuming, I was producing something of value, and I was still having fun. In fact, completing chapter after chapter was far more satisfying than floating around the mall to see what was on offer.

Maybe you *can* afford some help by releasing other spending that isn't so important to you.

Keep your eyes on the prize

Did you know that if you wrote 250 words a day; at the end of one year you would have written a full-length book? This 'Keep your eyes on the prize' section is 289 words long, so you can see it wouldn't take much to write it either.

You could write a book in a year by writing for no more than twenty minutes a day. That's what a lot of people don't realize; they overestimate what they can do in a month, but underestimate what they can do in one, two or five years.

Imagine if you slotted in a writing time attached to something else you habitually do, so that it was easy for you to remember to do it (until it became its own habit). If you always watch the news at 6 o'clock, set your writing time for 5.30pm. That will give you a little bit of time to settle at your computer, open the document and type for twenty minutes before you save your work a few minutes before 6 o'clock. Linking your new habit with an old, ingrained one will help embed it.

Or, you could get up half an hour earlier to write, before you have your shower and get ready for work. As I have already mentioned, this is my favourite time to write. I am still in my pyjamas and robe with fluffy slippers, and I take a big mug of tea into my office. I am usually stalked by our cats and dogs so I feed them too, then they join me at my desk for some writing time. It truly is my favourite time of the day.

When could you slot 20-30 minutes into *your* day for writing time?

Successful author action tips:

If you are serious about wanting to be an author, **take this chapter and apply it**.

Look at a typical day and **see where you can find an hour or half-hour to write**. Consider when you are most sharp – you will likely already know whether you are a morning or evening person.

Ask others for help and show them you mean business, by actually writing when you say you will.

Make it fun and enjoy what you do, then you will never have to push yourself.

Chapter 5
Create a motivating goal for yourself

Writing a book does not have to be a big, daunting task. You can make it fun and easy all by the way you look at it. Throw in an inspiring plan, and you're good to go.

I love to make my next book into an exciting project by giving myself a short deadline. Even if I don't make that deadline I still get far further than I would without it. Think about something completely crazy such as, 'I'm going to write a book in a week'. That's completely absurd, right? When people take years to write a book?

Diamonds are formed under pressure from plain old carbon. I want you to do the same with your writing. Take your thoughts, ideas, passions, interests, experience and the things you like to do, and put them through a pressure cooker situation to come up with an absolute diamond – your book.

Have a thrilling goal for your first draft

Why not write a book in a week, a month, or three months? I have written a book in a couple of weeks and I have also taken over a year. One of my first books, *Thirty Chic Days,* took many years, but most of that was self-doubt and not knowing what to do.

It is my sincere hope for this book that it extinguishes both self-doubt and not knowing what to do, so there is no such excuse for you not to write your book in good time.

A book doesn't have to be long either; I think that's the first hurdle to get out of the way. Some of my favourite non-fiction eBooks that I've bought from self-published authors have been quite short – less than fifty pages. This equates to about 15,000 to 20,000 words, which is not much when you consider that a full-length book is a minimum of 60,000 to 80,000 words, and some novels are well over 100,000 words.

I love using the word count function on my Microsoft Word program, because not only does it help me structure my books, but seeing those words pile up spurs me on too.

I've been planning on writing this book for quite a while – a 'how to write a book' book. Then, today, I became excited about it again and decided to give myself an unrealistic deadline – I would complete it in one week.

Here's how I worked it out so that my little mind would not be blown to bits. I had already decided on a length of around 40,000 words. I would break this up by writing at least twenty chapters of approximately 1,500 to 2,000 words each.

I started each chapter in a new Word document, so I could glance down to the bottom left corner of my screen from time to time and see how close I was to the 1,500 word target. Doing this is highly motivating. Once I had crossed the word-count finish line and then added my end of chapter 'tips' section, I would file that chapter in the 'Completed files' folder on my computer, and move on to the next chapter.

If you decided that you wanted to write a short eBook to start with, you could choose 20,000 words which would be ten or twelve chapters of 1,500 to 2,000 words each. Do you think you could brainstorm a dozen chapter ideas related to your book title? And then write an essay for each? Doesn't that sound quite realistic and possible instead of the lofty 'I want to write a book'?

Imagine if you decided on that and chose to write one chapter a day for two weeks. That even gives you a few days off. If you temporarily parked self-doubt and just did it, you could have a book ready to edit and upload to Amazon within a fortnight.

For the book you are reading, my initial plan was to write twenty chapters of at least 1,500 words for each. I would write four chapters a day over five days. That's huge for me. I wasn't planning on *publishing* it in a week, but the goal was to have the manuscript completed so I could then move on to editing and getting my cover designed.

In the end that short timeframe did not happen, but I certainly got a great start at this book and I don't regret my 'crazy' plan for one minute.

Sometimes it works well just to throw everything else out the figurative window and focus on the one thing that will write your book – writing your book! It clears all the mind clutter so that you can focus on... writing.

Working your goal into your schedule

Now that I am a full-time, work-from-home writer, I can write all day if I want to. Yes, I have tasks, errands and chores to do, but if I wanted to, I could clear the decks and work exclusively on my current book, only doing the household chores that absolutely must be done.

I did actually write the first draft of my book *Financially Chic* in a couple of weeks, because I was so fired up about the topic. I still worked with my husband Paul in our shoe store, but had just gone from five days a week, to four.

On work days I woke at 6am and wrote for an hour, before I had a shower and got ready to leave. If I had the day off, I'd write for most of the day and finish up in the afternoon in time to make dinner, and relax when Paul got home from work.

I work much better in the mornings and like to go to bed quite early (between 9pm and 10pm), plus I like to spend time in the evening chatting with Paul, so for all those reasons I don't write after dinner, but I used to in the early days. I had the laptop on our dining table and wrote while Paul watched television. We were still in the same room, so it felt companionable.

You could even write in your lunch break at work. If you felt okay about it or were happy to check that you could use your work computer – even though it's in your lunch break, you would still be using it for non-company purposes – you could type chapters and email them to yourself. Emailing your work is a quick and easy way to back up your writing, and have it accessible from anywhere – just save the emails as drafts.

It's the fire that counts

There really is no excuse any of us can come up with for not having the time to write. Sure, we all have lots going on, some more than others; but more often it's the motivation that helps us create the time. When you're lit up about what you are doing, you can't *not* do it. You love what you're writing about so much, that you fit in little pieces here and there. Before you know it you are past the half-way mark, then three-quarters and you are spurred on even more because you can see the finish line.

For me it's the middle of a book that lags, so I always make sure to keep my motivation stoked.

The first part of a new project is exciting. You've brainstormed the chapter titles and are getting a feel for the book. It's going to be so good! And off you go, out of the starting gates. Before you've reached halfway though, you might start feeling a little bogged down. 'I'll never finish!' you tell yourself. Hardly positive I know...

But then I remember my goal. I check out my schedule – four chapters a day for five days, and if I get ahead of myself I can do more than four in a day. This is my second chapter on the first day and it's 1.42pm. I will finish this chapter soon, and do two more before I clock off to start dinner around 5 or 5.30pm.

Sure, you may not want to keep this pace up every week, but to do it every so often and have written the first draft of your book? Why wouldn't you want to set a motivating goal for yourself with such a fabulous outcome?

Successful author action tips:

Please take this chapter seriously and don't just think, 'I'll look at it one day when I am more advanced/less busy etc'. Even if you are a brand-new author-to-be and haven't published anything yet, why not try it? What have you got to lose? I can't think of a more fun or satisfying way to kickstart my first book, even if it might feel unbelievably scary at the same time.

Choose a deadline that feels good to you and map out when you can write. You might do a word-count goal, or you could go for a 'write every day for one hour' goal. I find word-count goals more motivating but we're all different, so set a writing time goal if you can be sure you won't be distracted by Internet browsing and telephone calls.

Imagine that good feeling when you have completed all your chapters and are heading into the editing phase. Imagine seeing your completed cover which will bring your book to life. Imagine seeing it up for sale and then that there are people ordering it.

All these things are achievable and it's just a matter of going through them step-by-step, starting with your thrilling book goal. I know you can do it!

Chapter 6
My favourite way to structure my writing

I'm sure there are a million ways to structure your writing, and you could spend a lot of time studying all the different methods. For me, I like to keep things simple. I'd rather be writing my next book than finding the 'perfect' way of writing. If you keep on practicing, you are going to improve. And if you find yourself being a permanent student who doesn't stop studying long enough to actually apply what you learn... you probably won't get far.

When writing a non-fiction book, I love that you can create 'out of order', meaning you could start with the end, write the middle and then finish up with the introduction. I know it sounds like a child's storybook riddle, but it's true. You can write in whichever order you like. Let's start at the beginning and go through each step – in the correct order! – of how I write my books.

You will already have a list of possible book titles which you have come up with in *Chapter 2*, so let's choose one and get going.

Decide how long you want your book to be

When I wrote *Thirty Chic Days*, I had no idea how long a book was meant to be. That point really made me feel stuck, so I went on a hunt to find out how many words I would need. And how many pages? How *big* were the pages? I had so many questions!

I eventually found out that a normal non-fiction book contained around 60,000-70,000 words. Since my book format was inspired by my *30 Chic Days* blog series, I knew I wanted to have thirty chapters in this book.

From there it was a simple maths equation to work out that I needed to write approximately 2,000 words per chapter, multiplied by thirty chapters which gave me 60,000 words. In addition, I'd have extra words in my introduction, and the bonus chapter I planned to include.

With the book you have in your hands now, I decided I wanted it to be a shorter book, which was quick to read and implement. As I have previously mentioned, I settled on having twenty chapters of at least 1,500 words each and an end goal of between 30,000 and 40,000 words (it has ended up containing around 46,000 words).

To decide the length of your book, research how other books look. Choose a book from your shelves at home and see how many pages there are. Would you ideally like to write a book that size? Bigger? Smaller? Then grab a ruler and measure the cover. What physical size of book do you like? A big flappy one? A small, thick one? There is a list of common paper sizes on Amazon's self-publishing website kdp.com, and it would be helpful to choose one of those. Then, download the template that is offered and you can start your writing.

I decided that my larger books would be 5.5" x 8.5" and my smaller books 5" x 8".

Tip: On KDP you are looking for a 'Paperback Manuscript Template' and it's helpful to choose the 'Templates with sample content.'

Brainstorm a list of ideas to include

The next step is to start brainstorming your chapter titles and ideas.

For *Thirty Chic Days* I already had a list, because I had the blog series as a guide. But I still went through and brainstormed a list of thirty topics that went well with each other and gave a 'complete' overview of what I considered would comprise a chic life *a la Fifi*.

You could also ask yourself, 'What are the main important things I want my reader to know?'

I found this a helpful question to use for the book you are reading. I said, 'What are the twenty most important things I want my readers to know on the topic of writing a book and becoming an author?' As I noted down everything I wanted to share, I was creating an outline to work from at the same time.

Start writing

The resulting list from your brainstorming session is a great start in terms of chapter titles, and you can also note down any ideas for those topics. These will became subtitles and prompts for what to include in that chapter.

It doesn't matter that your ideas aren't in order – you will be able to move things around later, but for now, pick a chapter title that looks exciting or that you have something to say about, and start.

It's quite incredible but it really is that simple.

Your brainstormed list will be on one document, or as a hand-written list on paper. Once you have chosen the chapter you want to write first, put that at the top of a new Word document and start to type. As I have already mentioned in *Chapter 5*, I like to start a new

Word document for each chapter, because it makes it easier for me to see how many words I have typed for that chapter. It makes sense to me that my chapters would be similar in length, rather than a long chapter followed by two tiny chapters for example.

Then, once you have completed your chapter, tuck it away in a new 'Completed chapters' folder and move on to the next chapter.

Once you've banked your chapters

Once you have completed chapters for all the titles on your ideas list, the fun part is putting them together.

I open up the KDP 'Template with sample content' and begin cutting and pasting all those individual chapters into it. I like to choose 'Merge Formatting' if possible when adding the chapters in, as it saves me having to redo the formatting each time.

It would save a step if I typed straight into the book template, but I think it would slow down my creative process if I had to worry about keeping all the formatting correct. By typing on a normal Word document and not worrying about any formatting except for titles and subtitles, I can feel freer as I write.

Plus, I like to keep track of the word count for each chapter, as I have already mentioned.

As you start slotting each chapter into the template, replacing sample content, it's exciting. The document is starting to look like a book!

(One quick note before we carry on: if you are planning on publishing on Kindle only, you don't need to use the template. You can simply copy and paste all your chapters together into one big Word document with only the formatting you already had, and that is fine to upload as a Kindle book once you've finished editing.)

Once you have everything in one Word document you might start getting palpitations. It's such a big document! So overwhelming! But wait, here's where the Navigation feature of Word comes in.

The template will likely already have the chapters listed, but it if doesn't, or you are working from a Word document for 'Kindle only', read on.

In Microsoft Word, go to View, then tick the box next to the Navigation pane. I don't use Mac, but I've been told it should be the same in Word for Mac. Then click on Headings within the Navigation pane.

Next, go to References along the top, and, while having your cursor within the chapter title or highlighting the chapter title, click on Add Text. For your chapter titles choose Level 1, and your subtitles Level 2. It's up to you whether you add in Level 2 or not.

I tend to think that if you have a decent number of chapters, you can just go with Level 1 chapter titles, otherwise the table of contents could look overwhelming.

On the other hand, if you have decided on six main chapters, which are further broken down with five subtitles per chapter for example, you might want to include them as Level 2 under the Level 1 chapter titles. Otherwise, only listing six chapters in your table of contents could look a bit 'bare bones'. But hey, it's your book so you can do what you want. I have seen books where the author keeps a clean look, by listing only half-a-dozen main categories in the table of contents. It looks very simple and zen.

As you go through your book document and allocate Level 1 and Level 2 to chapter titles and subtitles, you will see them pop up in the Navigation pane. It's fun to view your table of contents being constructed before your eyes, and makes your book seem so real.

Another great thing about the Navigation pane is that you can reorder the chapters as you see fit, by simply dragging the chapter title up or down to reposition within the pane. All the subtitles and text associated with that chapter go along with it – *anything underneath the chapter title automatically transfers*. It's such a fantastic feature.

That's when you can work out a good flow to the layout of chapters, and hopefully when you start reading through your book to edit it, you will be excited and happy with what you see.

There will be more on editing in *Chapter 13*, but essentially as you go, you can tidy up references to other chapters and reword paragraphs to smooth the flow from chapter to chapter.

I like to use 'Chapter X' as a placeholder when I have referenced another chapter in the same book. It is an easy phrase to search for, and find those spots so that I can update them with the correct chapter number once I have decided the order, and title, if the title has changed.

In the past when I didn't use the 'Chapter X' phrase, I would only stumble across chapter mentions accidentally and it was a real worry that I would have an incorrect mention of another chapter in the book if I hadn't picked it up. By using 'Chapter X' I can search for that phrase to make sure I have updated all the mentions.

I have used the 'Chapter X' placeholder method writing this book, so hopefully you won't find any left over in the finished copy. If you do, please consider it good luck, much like finding the sixpence in a traditional Christmas pudding :)

Successful author action tips:

Don't feel too deflated at the thought of this chapter. I know it might sound complex and techy. It's not really bad though. Writing a book is simply a matter of following the process and **never giving up**. Plus, know that you are smart and can work things out. When I have worked out something I didn't previously know, such as how to use the Navigation pane, it felt like I'd conquered Mt Everest. It's wonderful to feel proud of yourself.

Don't let the demons get you either. Even as I write this chapter I am starting to feel like perhaps this book is a waste of time and that it doesn't need to be written. *'Who am I fooling? People will complain about this book!'*, I hear in my mind.

When that voice starts up, **remind yourself why you are writing your book in the first place**. Also, consider that it's not about you. It's about your reader, and you are selfish to even contemplate giving up, because then your reader might never get the message that only you can give them.

As long as you **write to the best of your ability** and endeavour to produce a quality product, there is no reason why you should listen to the doubting voices in your head – or from your family or friends.

Chapter 7
How to write

It seems funny to have a chapter on the process of writing, because it flows naturally for me. I just talk onto the screen through my fingers. I'll try and explain it though, because I understand that a 'how to write' chapter really is a necessity in a 'how to write a book' book.

After I had written and published a few books I saw advice on non-fiction writing that said to, 'write as you speak', and I thought, 'well I already do that – how convenient.' It just happened, likely from writing on a blog for many years. So that was a bonus I hadn't planned for.

You don't need to have any prior writing experience though, in my opinion. All that's required is a desire to write, and I can almost guarantee you have that. So let's talk about writing and how I approach it.

At its very simplest, I decide on the topic for a chapter (because I'll already have a list of ideas and chapter titles for my book), open up a new Word document and start typing. I continue typing until I reach the pre-decided word count I'm aiming for, and then round off the chapter with some kind of ending and possibly an 'action tips' section also.

You do this twenty or thirty times and *et voila*, you have a book!

Let's step back a bit though. How do we organize our thoughts to write?

Little pieces fall out of my head at all times of the day and night, especially if I'm focusing everything into finishing my current book. It helps to have a spiral notebook where I capture all those ideas, and if possible arrange them under separate topics or chapters.

These ideas give me jumping off points for a section, or even a whole new chapter. This 'how to write' chapter was added later in the book's development when I saw from reading through the table of contents that it felt like something was missing.

It's never too late to add a chapter into a book, even if you are in the editing process. It's your book and there is no definitive way to write it. Certainly, I would encourage you to read books on writing if you feel called to, but don't feel like you have to put your time in before you can write. Write now *and* learn as you go. You can only get better by doing; reading all the theory will not get your book(s) written. Why not do your theory and practical lessons (the writing) at the same time if that feels good to you.

When you need inspiration

It's recommended that writers read a lot, and I agree. But I'm sure you will find as I do, that it's not a hardship to read. I don't write every day, but I do read every day and have done my entire life. That's probably one common denominator among writers – we're all big readers. In fact, I'd think it would be a rare thing to find a writer who never read. After all, isn't it reading our favourite books that ignited a spark in us that we'd like to write a book too? Haven't we all dreamed of writing a book that excites the reader's imagination and stirs feelings in them?

If you find you need a little boost to kickstart your writing, either for the first time ever or perhaps for the day, open a book you love. It might be the same genre as you want to write in, or it might purposely be the complete opposite.

Take inspiration from that book. See how the author has started a chapter. I find that when I am reading a book for pleasure, I come across different ways of writing that I really admire. I don't copy them verbatim, but I do let them sink in and marinate so that my own writing can take on some of the flavour, or I might use what I've found out as a tip.

Sometimes it's a feeling I take from an author too. One author whose books get me motivated quite quickly, has a very fast-moving and excitable air to her words. Another author, who has written a book on creating your own spa time at home, uses words and phrases which are dreamy and quite hypnotizing. Just reading a few pages relaxes me. These books show me that you can indeed influence how your reader feels just by your writing. It's powerful stuff.

Your style will develop as you go

You can spark yourself off with others' work and then move into your own writing style as you practice. It really is a case of just doing it. The late Jackie Collins had a great quote where she said she didn't have writer's block, she had getting-to-the-desk block. I'm the same and I think many others might be too!

Just sit yourself down, open a blank Word document and start on a topic. There is advice that says you should choose an ideal reader and write to her, and sometimes I pick a reader I know and do that. But mostly I write for myself.

If I am explaining how to do something such as in this book, I'll proceed as if I am explaining my writing process to a student, for example. And if I am writing one of my inspirational books such as *Thirty Chic*

Days, it's simply brainstorming everything I could conjure up that I want to include in my rose-tinted and fabulous dream life.

When you start writing, type how you would speak. If you had a friend sitting across from you and they asked you to explain the chapter title, or they had phrased it as a question to you, just tell them. It really is the easiest way to sound natural. Pretend they actually asked you, 'What is your favourite way to structure your writing – can you walk me through it?' and you told them.

It is not a lot different to writing an email to someone. (Although there is a slight difference between writing an email and writing for a book, as I found when I tried to include information I had previously emailed someone in a chapter. It had to be completely rewritten as it just didn't sound right in a book context).

Be yourself

You don't have to second-guess yourself and bend your writing to try and please the reader. You will please your ideal reader most by being yourself. I sometimes notice when I order a self-published Kindle book that the author has tried to sanitize themselves to seem professional, and appeal to the broadest possible audience. All that ends up happening is that the book is hackneyed, clichéd and dull. Harsh words, I know, but sadly it's true.

The books I love the most are ones where the author has let a little bit of their crazy out. Not a ton, but just enough to give their writing a spark – their own flavour. That's when I really get caught up in their world and loving them, and wishing they were my friend by the end of the book.

For me it works well to let a little bit of my crazy out too. I have ideas that inspire me, and I try to explain them in a simple and fun way with a touch of humour too. It's another example of the 80/20 rule – 80% normal, 20% completely nuts. Your writing has enough spice to be interesting, yet is relatable enough that people want to read more.

I can't think of any books that are completely cuckoo (perhaps because I couldn't get through the sample, let alone order them for full consumption), but I can recall blog posts where the writer was completely unfiltered, and it was frustrating to read. Their thoughts were scattered everywhere, and they came across as almost unhinged. (I'm sure I've been that person too though, so I'm not pointing the finger too much…)

It's a balance of letting the real you shine through, while still ensuring your thoughts are cohesive and understandable. It really is more an art than a science. Whichever way the words come together will form your style of writing and your 'voice' over time, and help you find your ideal readers.

Don't be a perfectionist

In the past when I have found myself stopping mid-flow and thinking, 'I've already used this word once in this paragraph, what's a better word to use?' I stop what I'm doing and go to thesaurus.com, putting the original word in to see if there is a similar but different word to use.

This is a great idea, but I've found it better to resist the urge and simply use the same word as before. Keep thesaurus.com for the editing stage at the end.

This goes against the perfectionist way of thinking that I, and so many others, suffer from. I say 'suffer' because being a perfectionist is stopping us from doing a lot of amazing things in life, including writing our book.

'If it's not perfect I may as well not bother'. That's exactly what editing is for though! For polishing up your writing, whether you do it or someone else does.

Follow your passion

The main takeaway I want you to hear from this chapter is that you don't need to try too hard. All you need to do is find the topics you are most interested in, then talk about them through your fingertips.

Write about what inspires you, and what excites you. What lights you up and you can't stop typing? The great thing about writing your book is that you can explore your passions in private. You don't need to worry about what your reader will think, since your book hasn't been published yet.

I like to tell myself that I can delete a chapter afterwards if it seems too personal or silly. That way I can feel liberated with my writing, and not feel constrained. And, I have never deleted a chapter in the final edit – more often when I read the book back to myself, I wonder what I was so worried about.

Successful author action tips:

Don't worry too much **about the mechanics of writing** and start out by *just writing*. Sure, pick up tips and make your writing as good as it can be, but please don't let the fear of not being good enough stop you from even starting. At its simplest, write about those topics which you have the greatest enthusiasm for, and you can't go wrong.

Write and stash. One day you'll begin outlining your book and then choosing a chapter to write. And then another chapter, and another. Once you have completed a chapter don't read back through it. Put it aside and start on your next chapter.

Don't read anything you've written until right at the end when you put everything together. *Then* you can start reading through your document as a whole. I promise you will be very pleasantly surprised at how much it resembles a book you'd quite like to read!

Be inspired by books you enjoy and write your own versions of those books. Be inspired by other authors. Naturally you will want to create your own phrases and sentences, and filter ideas through your own mind, but most everyone is inspired by someone else. Ideas you've read about in books will likely have come from other people, and the author is simply curating them through their own experiences and thoughts.

I am inspired by others thoughts too, but I mainly gain my inspiration from people in real life, movies, snippets of conversation, feelings, nature… so many things.

The more you notice what you're inspired by, the more will come to your attention.

Chapter 8
How would SHE show up?

One of the most fruitful and motivating exercises I have ever done (and continue to do, often) is the 'How would SHE (or HE!) show up?' I'm talking about that successful me who has already achieved what I want to achieve, whether it's completing my first book, losing weight, or decluttering my home.

I ask myself how that person would act, steps she would take, what she would think, her beliefs about her current goal… everything.

When I started writing my book *Thirty Chic Days*, I was frozen with the thoughts of:

Who are you to write a book?
It won't be good enough.

People will say it's rubbish.

I was never going to get going with judgements like that in my head. To counteract the negativity in my mind, I thought of all the ways a successful author would behave instead.

After all, to be an author you have to write and publish books, then show them to your ideal readers. By listening to the negative thoughts in my mind I was not going to get my books written and published, nor feel confident enough to promote them.

Find your motivation

When it comes to the 'How would SHE show up?' questions you ask yourself, frame them in the most motivating way possible for you. There are different angles to ask the same question, so write them out in various ways, and start to brainstorm from the question that gives you a fizzy, excited feeling inside.

For example, these are essentially the same questions:

How would a best-selling author show up?

How would a writer who earns $10,000 per month act?

What would a million-seller author do on a day-to-day basis?

How would an author who earns a good income while living a peaceful, chilled life act?

How would a number one New York Times author live her life?

Do any of these questions excite you? If yes, take that cue and start brainstorming. If not, ask yourself what would ring *your* bell?

For me, I pondered:

How would a successful, best-selling author behave? How does she show up, that successful author me? What daily actions does she take? How does she think?

And it started coming to me:

She writes regularly – every day – which would not only build up material for her books but improve her writing at the same time because practice makes perfect.

She ignores the critical voices in her head and simply writes.

She enjoys the process of writing, has fun doing it and writes about what she loves.

She asks herself: what is the message I most want to say to the world?

She spends quiet time coming up with new material.

She releases something new to purchase regularly.

She has an ongoing calendar mapping out her releases.

She keeps in touch with her audience.

She is upbeat, inspirational, aspirational, and real.

She has a clear vision for her message.

She has boundaries and is not available all the time/is available when she chooses to be.

She has mystique, and people want to know what she is going to say next.

She knows that being a successful author is readily available to her.

She is confident that she can do it and that she is worth it.

She inspires herself with positive mindset reading every day.

She creates solutions for people with her books.

She lives a life of high vibration and offers that to others.

She knows that she is safe today and always, and that there is nothing holding her back but herself.

She knows that her ideal readers will find her easily, if only she would honour her own desires and write and publish the books she adores.

She deeply and completely loves and accepts herself, no matter what.

(And, of course, if you are male, please feel free to replace the 'She' with 'He' in each example!)

This list is highly motivating to me, and you will find that your inspiration will give you an excited, happy feeling too. This good feeling will make it much easier to let yourself write and publish without too much internal censorship. Doing this lifts you up from the internal naysaying and thoughts of what other people might think of your work.

Be happy to be different to other people

Most people would never think to simply decide that they are going to be an author, but I know you are not most people. The simple fact that you are here reading this book tells me so. You want to do different things and live a different life to others.

You might have dreamed about it for years but wondered how it could ever happen. I know I did. When I worked in office jobs, I *knew* I was meant for something more creative, and I dreamed of the day when I could be at home more too.

Home is my favourite place to be and it was a wrench for me to leave for work each day. I know that sounds dramatic, but it was true! It seemed such a waste to me that a place I had paid for (whether it was rent or a mortgage), decorated in my favourite style and made lovely by cleaning and taking care of it should sit empty all week, while I pushed paper around in a boring office environment where everything was coloured grey or beige.

Don't get me wrong, the people I worked with were lovely and I have lifelong friends that I would never have met otherwise, but I felt as if my life was slipping away one boring day at a time. When 5pm came around it was as if I had been set free for the day and I couldn't wait to get home to feel joy again – to see my pets, water my outdoor plants, potter in the kitchen, peruse my bookshelf with pleasure, and entertain friends and family.

Yes, going to a job really got in the way of me living my life but of course it was highly necessary because, well, you need an income to live. At the same time, I really didn't want to wait until the usual retirement age of 65 to feel true freedom.

We only get one go at this life and if we sit around doing the same as everyone else because it feels too uncomfortable to do otherwise, we could end up wasting our life away.

Doing something different such as leaving your job because you now have an ongoing income from the books you write will feel exhilarating and terrifying at the same time. And it's not really that terrifying, just mildly scary. After all, you can always go and get another job if you want to, so why not aim for self-employment and try it out?

Infusing real life with your ideal inspiration

Now let's go back to our 'How would SHE show up?' list. As well as lifting our spirits and helping us believe that we can actually make this 'crazy' life change, can you see how it is a wonderful blueprint on what to do to make it happen?

For me I look at this list and see that I have to commit to writing daily, no matter how much self-doubt I might be feeling. Because you can be inspired all you want, but if you don't take actual action, nothing changes. This is often a shocking realization for those of us who live in their heads a lot of the time.

Read through your list (or mine if you haven't written yours yet) and decide on some inspired actions.

For me it means:

I will write daily, even if only for fifteen minutes.

I will start a file on my computer where I note down what I love to write about, and brainstorm book idea after book idea.

I will research things I need to know about.

I will keep in touch with my audience regularly.

I will keep an upbeat, happy feeling while I write.

I will inspire myself with positive mindset reading (and listening) every day.

Basically, it comes down to writing daily, whether it's for a book, a blog or social media post, or in my journal. I have found that the more I write, dream and design, the more that flows from my creative mind. You can't use your creativity up. In fact, the *less* you do, the less you'll get and the *more* you do, the more you'll get.

Your creative mind is a never-ending, abundantly flowing spring and by calling on it, you are keeping the pump primed, creating momentum and expanding your writing in a beautiful way.

Successful author action tips:

Find your own motivating questions and brainstorm inspiration for yourself. Dream big, don't censor, and have this as your own secret garden to inspire yourself to great things.

If it feels silly, instead **dream in a different, perhaps more practical way.** Some days my writing is flowery and flighty-headed, and other days it is very down-to-earth. Honour both sides of yourself and, as you give yourself permission to write about anything you like, you will find your writing style, topics and voice emerging.

To you your writing will just sound like 'you', but to your ideal readers **it will be enchanting**. 'It's like a sweet and caring friend talking to me', are the kind of comments my readers have shared, which makes me so happy. You will find the same when you give yourself permission to show up as you are and write from the heart.

> ***Tip:** My favourite success tip is to keep your frequency high with affirmations, journaling work, the 'How does she' exercise (it's so inspiring!) and write, write, write – your book, on your blog, posting on social media.*
>
> *Those two things will propel you forward quickly!*

Chapter 9
How to get past your fears

A major part of achieving success as an author – even more so than doing the work sometimes – is having the tenacity to overcome your blocks and fears: to write despite the critical words in your head and the feeling of uneasiness as you expand your comfort zone. These intangible thoughts can freeze you in your tracks if you let them.

I can't count the number of autobiographies, interviews and magazine articles I've seen where the celebrity/ author/ singer/ performer/ entertainer/ famous person has confessed that they still worry whether they're good enough for all the accolades.

This is both good news and bad news. Bad news just in case you thought that one day you'd magically wake up, and the negative voice in your mind had packed up and left town. Good news because you can be assured that self-doubt is an entirely human condition and pretty much *everyone* has it, or has had it, at some stage.

Or you might be like I was, waiting for someone to discover me. Right from day one of my blog I was convinced that I would be singled out by a book industry bigwig who happened upon my writing. I didn't think this in an 'I'm so great' way, more of a movie plot dreamworld kind of way. I waited for the email to arrive in my Inbox from a major publishing house offering me a three-book deal because they thought my writing was so amazing.

One day I realized if that never happened, was I willing to give up on my dream of becoming an author? Of course, the answer was no! And, as I have already mentioned, once I took the first step and published my own work, I *did* receive emails from companies wanting to publish my books – in other languages.

That's what you have to realize about self-publishing books (versus, say, working in a job). You will get out what you put in, but you have to do the work first. You have to write the book *before* you get the reward. But after that? The sky is the limit. No-one offered me a book contract before I'd written my first book, but now I have several from three different publishing houses.

This chapter is about mindset, and you will see as you go that a good mindset makes the writing part so much easier. You are far better to have a mindset that works with you, not against you.

Having a fearful and doubting frame of mind is like driving around in a car that not only has the handbrake on, but a wheel clamp too! You'll have a hard time driving around the corner, let alone getting into town.

Being influenced by their fears is what prevents most people from realizing their dream of being an author. They think their fears are real. It's tragic because they are anything *but* real. They literally are figments of our imagination, and the only person who can get rid of them is us.

It is *our* job to train our mind, much like we would a puppy. We can't let the puppy lead us around; we'd never complete our walk! It's the same with our mind. If we only do what our mind wants us to do, we'll probably end up sitting on the sofa with a tub of bon-bons, promising ourselves we'll start writing tomorrow.

You will be pleased to hear that once you know the right way to go about directing your mindset, it isn't that hard. Sure, you might have a few stubborn thoughts that pop up repeatedly, but when you've addressed them the first time, they aren't as big the next time. And each time they come up after that, they'll shrink smaller and smaller.

I can remember how I felt before I started writing, even on my blog. I was so keen to do something – write and be an author – but I also felt paralyzed. I didn't know what to do and I had no-one running in the track in front of me to show me that it was even possible.

I didn't know any writers or authors in real life, and the proper writing world seemed too serious and grown-up for me. Then when I saw that people were publishing their own books on Amazon, anticipation lit up inside me. Maybe this was something I could do too, I thought.

It wasn't all easy though; I procrastinated for long stretches of time and temporarily gave up often. But I kept getting pulled back by my desire of being an author. I loved writing so much that I knew it was the path for me. Looking back now, I can see that I would have progressed so much quicker if I had done more of the mindset work, at the same time as the action of writing my first book.

Addressing your fears

A big part of why we hold ourselves back from success is fear. Our mind wants to keep us safe, and that's why it plants fear as a block to keep us in the status quo.

Imagine if you had a toddler whom you wanted to keep safe (as we all would). The lazy way would be to have your toddler held in a playpen until she had grown up; that way nothing dangerous could ever happen to her. Of course, she'd never learn different things or stretch her mind, but at least she'd be safe.

That's what our mind wants for us. It's fearful, and a

little bit lazy. If we follow what everyone else around us does and take the usual life path, our mind is happy. It can predict what is going to happen next and for decades to come, because there is evidence all around that people have already done this. It's easy to see far, far into the future.

But maybe we want to follow our dreams and work from home as a writer, putting our private thoughts out into the public. Our mind will go berserk. 'Whaaaaat!' it screams, 'That crazy Fiona, she's wanting to be an author now. I've gotta stop her! Help!'

When you start taking action to achieve your biggest goals, your mind will do everything in its power to keep you in that safe, status quo place. It wants you locked up in the ease and safety of the playpen.

And this is when the terrible trio of fear, doubt and worry come in. They pop up more when you are growing yourself and doing different things. When you are sitting in the status quo, they happily sit quietly, but if you decide to do something a bit different, to push yourself to a new place, they are roused – big-time.

'Who do you think you are?' the terrible trio says.

'This is too risky.'

'It will never work.'

'What will others think?'

'You could be putting yourself in danger.'

I have found that a great way to stare fear, doubt and worry down is to ask them what they have to say. For me, it came up a lot that what I write about is silly, frivolous and unimportant when there are so many more serious things going on in the world.

But when did that ever stop anyone writing a happy story, filming a romantic comedy movie or writing a love song? Doesn't the world crave something fun and light? I know I do.

Other fears I had were:

- *It would be dangerous to have my surname in public – would strange people find out where I lived and turn up at my door?*

- *People would laugh at me or mock me for what I had written.*

- *People would judge what I wrote and use it against me.*

- *I might write something that would inadvertently get me into trouble.*

Doing something different such as publishing a book feels big and scary to your mind, so you can hardly blame her for wanting to keep you safe.

When you hear a bump in the night and immediately freeze, holding your breath so that you can hear better to tell if someone is in the house, what immediately dispels your fear? That's right, turning the lights on. When you see your cat sitting up on the desk having knocked a book off it, your fear dissolves instantly.

Listing all your fears, doubts and worries is invaluable, because it shines a light on them and shows you how silly they really are. When they are floating around in your head, it is easy to believe them. But when written down or spoken out loud, you can see they are nothing to be frightened of at all, or alternatively you can take steps to alleviate them. Fear has no chance of surviving this common-sense approach.

Successful author action tips:

Write down **every single reason** why you haven't written and/or published your book yet. Every fear you can think of. Then, look at each one objectively and ask if it's even true. When you can see things written down, or even better, speak them out loud to yourself, you will see how ludicrous they really are. That's exactly what happened to me with my fears.

And, if there are fears which are justified, you can isolate them and **take measures which would help**. I have found that taking even tiny bits of action helped me feel better. When I wasn't doing anything to address my fears, they grew in my mind like the bogeyman in the dark.

Chapter 10
Write fast

Writing fast is one of my top success tips if you want to be an author. No doubt you've heard of people who have been working on their book for ten years (with no end in sight). Do you want to be one of those people? I don't. I want to get my books out there and be a published author. I want to strike while the iron is hot and write while I have the idea.

And that's the thing, you have to go with the creative energy. I'm sure you have experienced at least once in your life when you have been inspired to do something, done it straight away whilst riding the wave of enthusiasm, and completed that project. Maybe it was at work, or something seemingly minor at home such as organizing a cabinet in your kitchen on the spur of the moment. The time flew and you were thrilled with the results.

Writing fast is the same principle. You are starting off with your excitement and passion for a certain train of thought, and letting momentum carry you through. You stick with it and don't let yourself get distracted. You finish one chapter, then another and eventually you complete the book.

I have written both fast and slow and fast is always better. One big reason is that your writing is more cohesive when you're in the zone. Think about writing a book over, say, a year. You will change in that time – your thoughts and ideas will change, and you will have experienced new things. When you read through the book for your final edits, you may well find that the chapters are a little clunky – some don't quite mesh with others and that's because a different person wrote them. The longer a book takes to complete, the worse it is.

And I would be willing to bet that the longer a book takes to finish, the less likelihood there is of it ever being published. The simple reason is that it goes stale.

Imagine if you started chopping vegetables for Christmas dinner and it was only February. You thought it would be a good idea to get a head start and do some each week so you wouldn't have to do it all in December. Would those vegetables look any good ten months later? Unlikely.

Ideas are the same. You can't let them hang around forever because they will lose their zing. Keep your energy fresh and plan to use it all up at once; don't keep it around for later.

(In *Chapter 4* when I talk about writing 250 words a day and at the end of the year you'd have a full-length book, that certainly is doable, but it isn't something I'd do myself. For me, it's far too slow, but it is a great illustrative point that shows it is not impossible to write a book with seemingly no available time. And, I'm sure someone, somewhere has done it with success! Or, perhaps, by writing a little bit every day you do stay in that zone, and have a fantastic book by the end of the year.)

Trick yourself into finishing your book

Another benefit of writing fast is that your logical brain won't be able to keep up. When your logical brain gets involved, you'll hear yourself say things such as:

This is no good; who are you trying to kid?

This topic has been written about a million times before.

People will laugh at you, mock you and give you one-star reviews if you even think about publishing this rubbish.

All of these things could be true, whether you publish your book or not. There *will* be people who think your work is a pile of poo. You *will* likely get some one-star reviews. You *will* have people mock your work and what you are writing about has *definitely* been done before.

I'm sorry to burst your bubble but it's true!

However, do you think that stopped JK Rowling, Sophie Kinsella, Dan Brown, Marie Kondo or any other successful author from continuing with their writing? All these writers have received scathing one-star reviews and a rubbishing from critics at one time or another. Do you think they care though? Or, as my mum says, are they crying all the way to the bank? When their books were optioned for movies and television programs, did they worry about those one-star reviews then?

When Marie Kondo shared her passion for tidying up, do you think people saying she was a bit cuckoo stopped her writing about thanking her clothes for their service and putting away her handbag for a 'rest' at night? I'm guessing not, because she published her book and others, and now has her own series on Netflix. Go Marie.

You are no different to any of these authors. You may even be a better writer than you are – I read Dan Brown's *The Da Vinci Code* and couldn't understand why it was so popular. Yes, it was a real page turner, but the writing was so basic. Same with the *Jack Reacher* books by Lee Child. I started reading the latest one because I thought all the hype must mean they were good. But the writing was so annoying I couldn't get past page twenty.

I'm sure Lee is very concerned that Fiona Ferris from New Zealand doesn't think his book is any good, because last time I looked he'd sold millions of copies – 100 million actually – and Tom Cruise plays his lead character role in the movie adaptations.

If you don't believe me that rich, famous, popular authors still have their detractors, go and look up a few of their titles on Amazon and read the one-star reviews. Some even have a larger percentage of one-star reviews than any other rating!

The thought that their work is no good did not stop these and many other authors, and that's why it is so important to trick your logical mind by writing fast. Don't give it a chance to pull you back. Imagine if you were guaranteed to have a number-one bestseller within a year or two, simply by writing and publishing your work. No-one knows for sure, of course, but it could happen. Marie Kondo's book took off very quickly. But if you never finish your book, it's 100% guaranteed *not* to happen. At least give yourself a chance, buy the admission ticket!

Your writing will be better

You may be thinking, sure, Fiona, I get all your persuasive points so far, but wouldn't it be better to take my time and make my writing really, really good, rather than rush things and possibly do a sub-standard job?

No, I don't believe it's possible to do a worse job by writing fast. In fact, the opposite will happen. You will be so caught up in enthusiasm for your book, that ideas will flow with ease, building on each other. You won't be worrying so much about the perfect word for that sentence and other words will come instead. You can always change them later while editing if you want.

You may even find yourself becoming quite giddy as I do. It almost feels as if I have a glass of champagne on my desk and I've been sipping from it because I do feel a little drunk. Drunk on words!

There is a famous quote often misattributed to Ernest Hemingway which says to, 'write drunk and edit sober'. I do think this has a lot of merit, but you can make yourself drunk on fun ideas rather than alcohol, by writing fast and not filtering or censoring what is flying through your fingertips.

To borrow from literature again, it's like Peter Pan. He keeps himself flying in the air by believing; when he stops believing, he falls to the ground. Trust in yourself enough to keep writing fast and don't look down. As I am writing this, if I stop writing and start thinking rationally about something, the magic falls away and I have to get myself back into the zone again.

Unleash your enthusiasm

It's actually easier to write fast than not – can you feel in this chapter the energy that's jumping off the screen or the page? It's almost palpable isn't it? And that's what I sense when I am reading a book whether it's fiction or non-fiction – the author's energy and enthusiasm for their story or topic.

When you are moving quickly there is naturally more energy, whether it's going for a walk, doing your housework or writing. Harness that magic and let it out in your writing by moving quickly.

I take a breather between chapters, but I try to always write one chapter as a complete piece, and that can only be done by writing fast, because I get bored easily. If I was told I had to write a chapter in, say, five hours, I would struggle. If I was given forty minutes, I would be much happier and do a better job too. I always go back and polish chapters later, but getting it down first is imperative.

Remember from *Chapter 5* that a diamond is produced out of carbon under extreme pressure, and that the same pressure is very useful in mining the diamonds from our mind? We're after champagne and diamonds darling, champagne and diamonds. They will lead you to success when you are writing your book.

Successful author action tips:

Dive into your writing when it feels good. Sometimes it won't be the most convenient time, but you've got to capture the magic while it's alive. I have done all of these things at one time or another:

- Dashed to my computer straight from the shower in my towel to get some paragraphs and thoughts down.
- Made a voice recording on my iPhone when out.
- Sent myself an email if my laptop is not nearby.
- Made some notes on a scrap of paper whether it's bullet points, book ideas or complete sentences.

Most often I don't wait for my muse, I just start writing to get myself into the zone, however when she appears I put everything down and listen to her. My husband is used to me pausing a movie and dashing up from the sofa to jot down some notes!

If you need a few prompts, here they are:

- Write what you're in the mood for. Your writing will flow beautifully.
- Remember that you don't have to write your chapters in the order they will be published in.

There is such freedom in being able to dive into the middle.

- And also remember, there is no such thing as writer's block; just write, and write fast.

Go and check out those one-star reviews of your absolute favourite authors and remember that everyone has them when your logical mind is stopping you. Don't let the thought of your work being 'not good enough' slow you down (because there's no such thing); look at those thoughts as kindling to build the fire in your belly.

Visualize your book up on Amazon whenever you need a boost to get your writing speed up. Hurry! People are waiting to order your book!

Chapter 11
The flow of your book and 'extras'

It is helpful to consider the format or structure of your book, a) to know how to lay it out, and b) because it breaks down a daunting task ('write a whole book') into easier to consider pieces ('fill in the gaps').

With your book you will have 'the book' of course, which is the main content –the chapters and possibly an introduction. Then there are all the extras such as the table of contents, 'other books by', and 'about the author' among others.

After writing several books I have come to a format which works for me. My books are not identical in their makeup, but they do follow a similar format. Again, it's to be cohesive between my titles, plus it gives me a kind of template to work with as I patchwork my books together, because that's what it is, right? You write this piece and that piece and put them all together, hopefully in the end creating a beautiful work of art.

Some authors put a lot of other extras in their books such as cross-promotion, reviews, excerpts of other books and media mentions. I don't put those extras in my books which is just my preference. Personally, I like a clean reading experience, so I want to give this to my reader as well.

With your book, it's *your book* though, so you can put in as few or as many extras as you want to. One self-published author whose books I enjoy puts an introduction, ten chapters and then her standard 'About the Author' and 'Others Books by' at the end. That's all. You really can make things as simple or as complex as you want.

The general flow of my books is as follows:

Title pages
Dedication (optional)
Other books by Fiona Ferris
Table of contents
Introduction
Chapters
Bonus chapter (optional)
Bonus list of ideas (optional)
A final word (optional)
About the author
Book bonuses

The great thing with extras too, is that you don't have to write them new each time. 'Other books by Fiona Ferris' has books added to it whenever I write a new title. 'About the Author' is not updated for every new book, but I do update it every so often. And 'Book Bonuses' is mostly the same with an occasional update as well.

Let's start with why I don't put some items in my books that other authors can do. I don't like either of these things for the following reasons (but I do reserve the right to change my mind at any time. It seems that as soon as I say I don't like something, I want to do it. Call me contrary.)

Praise/reviews for their book or previous books

When a book starts off with page after page of praise (some go on forever), it grates a little. Firstly, I'm anxious to get reading but I have to wade through all this other stuff. And secondly, I've already bought the book, so please stop selling it to me!

It also comes across as self-promotion – that the author is tooting their own horn too much, but this may be more to do with my down-to-earth Kiwi upbringing. For instance, I know the North American culture is a lot more confident with promoting themselves, which I think is great. I could certainly use a little more of that, but I have to go with what feels right for me.

And it's the same for you – you get to choose what you do in your books so if you want to talk yourself up, promote away.

A preview of another of the author's books

My second pet peeve is the preview of another book at the end of a book. I get it, it's a great idea. Why not start your reader off on the next in the series or another of your books and hopefully they'll want to order that one too. But when I am 74% or 88% into my Kindle book and really enjoying it, it's upsetting to arrive at the end not long after and a preview comes up. I thought I still had quite a bit of the book to go, and now I feel ripped off!

To offer readers a preview of my other books I provide a 'Book Bonuses' page in each of my books where they can join my email list. They are then automatically sent an excerpt from each of my books to download and read.

However, I am all for trying new things, so who knows, maybe one day you'll order one of my books and find an excerpt of my next book at the end. Just as you are free to choose what you put in your books, you are also free to change your mind at any moment.

Now let's move on to what extras I *do* like to put into my books, starting with:

'Bonus chapter'
'Bonus list of ideas'

It always feels good to me to put one or two bonus extras in my books. Sort of like when you buy a makeup product and they throw a few samples in the bag too. It leaves the customer with a sense of generosity and good feeling. The way an author can do this is with a bonus chapter or checklist.

How can you tell what is a normal chapter and what is a 'bonus' chapter though? In the case of my books *Thirty Chic Days, Thirty Slim Days* and *Thirty More Chic Days*, it's easy, because I had… yes, thirty chapters/days, and then a bonus chapter/day after that.

In a book where the number of chapters isn't specified in the title (and let's face it, most fall into that category), you can still denote a chapter as a bonus by placing it right at the end and introducing a new topic or recapping everything covered in the book – like a summary of all the chapters. I haven't done a summary or checklist bonus chapter yet, but these appeal a lot, so I will keep them on my list of 'ideas to try'.

A compilation of inspiring concepts is one I love too. At the end of my book *Financially Chic*, there is a list called '100 Ways to be Financially Chic'. This chapter took me quite a while as I brainstormed in chunks and I really had to stretch my mental resources to come up with one hundred items, but I have had such great feedback on that chapter (and it *is* a good chapter) so it was all worth it.

It's a quick and punchy list to get the reader motivated to start putting into practice simple and easy ideas once they finish the book. I love the '100 Ways' idea so much that I have used it in other books such as in *Thirty More Chic Days* where it is called '100 Ways to be Chic'.

If doing something like this appeals to you, you could call it:

100 Ways to...
50 Top Tips to...
25 Inspiring Ideas to...

You don't have to create this chapter right at the end either. Imagine if you started off your book by writing this chapter. You would brainstorm a ton of ideas and provide some great momentum for yourself.

Alternatively, when I wrote it after completing the book, it was useful to provide little summaries of all the ideas in the book.

'A final word'

I love to leave my readers with an encouraging word at the end too, much like I am writing them a letter. Even if I wrote fiction, I would still probably do this. It feels good to thank them for reading my book and to give a last pop of enthusiasm. I sign it off with my name, just as I would in a letter.

I didn't do this in my earlier books but now that I've finished a few books this way, I'm hooked. It feels personal and I will probably continue this idea with future books.

'Other books by Fiona Ferris'

All authors who have more than one title will have somewhere in their book which mentions those other books. I like to put mine on one page, at the front, before the table of contents.

To save time and give my books a unified look, I have templates for sections such as 'Other books'. As I mentioned before, I add in new books as they are written.

Then, when I go to publish a book, I copy and paste the relevant (Kindle or print) list, and remove the title of the book which its going into. For example, for my book 'Financially Chic', I would remove the 'Financially Chic' entry from the list.

Here is my working document which I copy and paste into the relevant manuscript:

For Print:

Other books by Fiona Ferris

Thirty Chic Days: *Practical inspiration for a beautiful life*

Thirty More Chic Days: *Creating an inspired mindset for a magical life*

Thirty Slim Days: *Create your slender and healthy life in a fun and enjoyable way*

Financially Chic: *Live a luxurious life on a budget, learn to love managing money, and grow your wealth*

How to be Chic in the Winter: *Living slim, happy and stylish during the cold season*

A Chic and Simple Christmas: *Celebrate the holiday season with ease and grace*

The print version, previous, has normal writing, and the Kindle version, below, has live links and a smaller font for the heading (I explain why I use smaller fonts in *Chapter 15*).

For Kindle:

Other books by Fiona Ferris

[Thirty Chic Days](#): Practical inspiration for a beautiful life

[Thirty More Chic Days](#): Creating an inspired mindset for a magical life

[Thirty Slim Days](#): Create your slender and healthy life in a fun and enjoyable way

[Financially Chic](#): Live a luxurious life on a budget, learn to love managing money, and grow your wealth

[How to be Chic in the Winter](#): Living slim, happy and stylish during the cold season

[A Chic and Simple Christmas](#): Celebrate the holiday season with ease and grace

---

About the author

Your 'About the Author' page can be tough to write, which is why I'd recommend doing it before or while you are writing your book. Trust me, the last thing you will feel like doing when you finish your book is still to have an 'About the author' blurb to write. When I did it this way, I felt as if I had no words left in my head.

Write your 'About the author' piece when you are in a good mood too – when you are feeling sparky, and even a little bit silly. Draft a few different versions or just pour your thoughts out, then edit the piece down to two or three paragraphs.

Have a look through books you own, or online at Amazon, and see what other authors have written about themselves. Take inspiration from bios that appeal to you and then make up your own version of them.

Here is my current blurb, but in writing this chapter I feel inspired to make a change, so who knows, when this book is published there may be a completely different 'About the author' page at the back of it – or not, if I've run out of brain power.

As with my 'Other books by', my 'About the author' print and Kindle versions have different links – written out for the paperback and as clickable 'live' links for the eBook.

About the Author

Fiona Ferris is passionate about, and has studied the topic of living well for more than twenty years, in particular that a simple and beautiful life can be achieved without spending a lot of money.

Fiona finds inspiration from all over the place including Paris and France, the countryside, big cities, fancy hotels, music, beautiful scents, magazines, books, all those fabulous blogs out there, people, pets, nature, other countries and cultures; really, everywhere she looks.

Fiona lives in the beautiful and sunny wine region of Hawke's Bay, New Zealand, with her husband, Paul, their rescue cats Jessica and Nina and rescue dogs Daphne and Chloe.

To learn more about Fiona, you can connect with her at:

howtobechic.com
fionaferris.com
facebook.com/fionaferrisauthor
twitter.com/fiona_ferris
instagram.com/fionaferrisnz
youtube.com/fionaferris

For Kindle:

About the Author

Fiona Ferris is passionate about, and has studied the topic of living well for more than twenty years, in particular that a simple and beautiful life can be achieved without spending a lot of money.

Fiona finds inspiration from all over the place including Paris and France, the countryside, big cities, fancy hotels, music, beautiful scents, magazines, books, all those fabulous blogs out there, people, pets, nature, other countries and cultures; really, everywhere she looks.

Fiona lives in the beautiful and sunny wine region of Hawke's Bay, New Zealand, with her husband, Paul, their rescue cats Jessica and Nina and rescue dogs Daphne and Chloe.

To learn more about Fiona, you can connect with her at:

howtobechic.com
fionaferris.com
facebook.com/fionaferrisauthor
twitter.com/fiona_ferris
instagram.com/fionaferrisnz
youtube.com/fionaferris

Book bonuses

Providing book bonuses is a great way to provide extra value for your readers at the same time as asking for their email address. You can then keep in touch with your newsletter or blog post, and let readers know about future books as you release them.

I use Mailchimp for my email list and have set up an autoresponder to send out my 'Welcome' email automatically. This includes excerpts of my books and 'other chic goodies' (a PDF and audio of a short piece I wrote called '21 Ways to be Chic').

Mailchimp is free to use until you reach 2,000 subscribers and it has many great features like the autoresponder. It took me years to get to 2,000 subscribers, so I had lots of free value while my list grew.

You can include whatever you want as an enticement for readers to join your mailing list, and you can use the same 'carrot' as your 'Book Bonuses' link.

Whenever I create a new 'lead magnet' (which is the official term), I add it to the others, so whenever people join my mailing list, they get a lovely big list of freebies.

Some authors include just their latest free offering, while others have several different lead magnets all attached to the same mailing list. For me at the moment, I prefer to keep things simple and just have the one link with all my offers on it.

Just like your chapters, you can write your extras out of order too. You don't necessarily have to wait until the end when you need them, but it's a nice feeling to have already completed them when you finish your book and are ready to edit.

As with your 'About the author' profile, to then be told that you still have to write all those things at the end would almost be too much. Because even though writing is definitely fun and enjoyable, it's also a little bit taxing just like any other job.

That's why you want to keep the ball rolling and not simply wait for the muse to strike. It's a combo deal really – part inspiration, part perspiration; just like the motivational framed print from the 1980s says.

Successful author action tips:

This chapter is about creating the extras that will stay the same in each of your books such as 'About the author', 'Other books by…' and 'Book bonuses' etc.

Then, consider with each book you write what your bonus chapters will be, if you include them. Write at least one thing that is called 'Bonus' because it really does feel different. Give your readers that little bit extra and **have fun putting it together**.

Chapter 12
The hidden benefits of exploring your author fantasy

Something I have only just begun to see after writing for a while are the fantastic benefits of being an author. Writing books lets you discover more about yourself, find out what makes you happy, and learn how you can feel more fulfilled in your life.

When you are writing, you're tapping into your dream self – your subconscious. By drawing out all those golden threads of happiness, which after all is what you will naturally want to write about, you are not only creating a new career for yourself, but you are delighting yourself at the same time.

Finding out what lights you up

For me it applies as a non-fiction writer, because I adore writing about creating a beautiful life without spending a lot of money; having a positive mindset; enjoying femininity and creativity; and creating personal success. All my books have these common themes and I get to write about them in as pretty and fanciful way as I desire. (That same flossy way of thinking which meant some of my family members laughed at words I used, or how I choose to decorate my life.)

For you it can apply to your favourite topics, or even if you wanted to write fiction. Imagine creating your dream world on paper and being recognized for it. Imagine writing down your favourite inspiration or *exactly* the story you'd love to read, and others fell in love with your ideas too. Imagine if this could be your *job*.

Recently I ordered a set of headboards for our guest room from a small local bed factory. As I was speaking with the lady serving me about the size of the bed, the owner of the factory whom I'd originally bought the bed itself from walked past and said, 'Hi Fiona', and then to his staff member, 'This lady is an author'. After a few minutes conversation the woman serving me had a dreamy look in her eyes and told me how she'd done a bit of writing in her favourite genre of fantasy fiction.

It turned out the only reason she hadn't done

anything with her writing was self-doubt: *Was it good enough?* she wondered. But isn't that for the reader to decide? If you have done as good a job as you can, and read through and edited your book to ensure it flows well and isn't saturated with errors, then surely it's not up to you to decide if it's good enough?

She really did have such a palpable excitement and happiness for the genre she loved to read, and even said, 'I've run out of books from my favourite authors'. 'Start your own series then! Write the books you want to read!', I was almost squealing with enthusiasm to her.

I really hope she takes that first step, because I know she'd have a super-fun time writing her dream books, and she'd also not have to work in a bed factory. When I said I work from home writing books she almost swooned, 'I'd love that'. And it's not beyond the realms of an ordinary person, as I have found out. You can start in a low-risk way, by starting to write on the side of your full-time job.

A personal record for posterity

Another benefit of writing your own books is that you essentially end up with journals of your past thoughts, dreams and ideas. When I recently updated my book covers of titles already published, I took the opportunity to read through each book one at a time and do another spelling and grammar sweep. I was tempted to update parts of my books where my life was different now, but then I had the conundrum that I'd have to change other parts of the book too. This led me to think that I'd then be rewriting the whole book, which was not the intention. In addition, those books are perfectly encapsulated moments in time, which perhaps some readers might need to read exactly as they are.

As humans we are always evolving, so it makes sense that as we write, our books will change and grow with us. If I wrote another version of the book you are now reading in twenty years' time, the latter would likely be more advanced or perhaps assume that the author knows more, since I would have forgotten everything I had gone through and how I had to be when I was first starting out.

For the beginner author-to-be, the earlier title is likely to be so much more helpful, which is why you don't need to wait until you are an 'expert' to write your book. Write now and share what you have learned to date. You will not only help someone who needs your words *today*, you will also have the benefit of crystallizing all your current knowledge and experience.

The occasional time I pick up one of my own books and read a chapter, I am often surprised that I don't remember that I wrote it *at all. How is that possible?* I think, but then I rationalize it to myself. *Well, we can't remember everything perfectly*, and that's why it's nice to have written records of your thought process at that time. *'Writing: it's not just for the reader!'*

Successful author action tips:

Write what makes you happy. Do you think someone who loves to cook and tinker with new recipes would enjoy sharing those recipes? Yes! What about someone who loves reading political thriller books and often guesses the clues; do you think they would come up with new and exciting plot ideas? I think so.

Whatever you are most passionate about reading is your perfect subject for writing, and because you already love it, it will make you even happier! I've never written a fiction book, but I've written small pieces for myself, and I know that one day (maybe soon!) I will have a go at writing the book I most imagine myself enjoying reading. Just thinking about it gives me excited flutters in my tummy!

Give yourself the gift of a personal journal.
Imagine what a thrill it would be to have your recent history chronicled in books. Whether it's fiction or non-fiction, there will be pieces of you – your mental DNA – in your writing.

Then, years later you can enjoy recalling your thoughts of that time.

Write for like-minded people. Through my blog, books and social media, I have met (mostly virtually, but a few in real life), the kindest and most creative women I could ever conjure up, and been inspired by the various ways they live. Not many other hobbies can offer that, and if you paid for the introduction to a friend finder or match maker, you probably still couldn't find acquaintances so perfect for you.

And the other side applies too; when I am writing my books, I often have these ladies – my ideal readers – in mind.

It's not true that only sad, lonely people sit at home behind their computer. Yes, I like to get out and meet people in my everyday life, but I have met wonderful friends and gained a real sense of community by sharing my interests and passions online, and in my books.

Chapter 13
How to edit your book

Let's change gears now, and get into the practical skill of editing your work. As I trained myself to edit, I saw that writing and editing are two very different processes, and it's best to do them separately. If you try to do both at the same time, you will likely do neither well.

Writing involves your creative brain, and this is when it is beneficial to slip into an almost dream-like state. When I am writing, I suspend my critical mind and just go with it. I don't judge what is coming out onto the screen, and I let fanciful words and ideas flow.

You will interrupt your creativity if you try to write and edit at the same time, so don't worry too much about clunky sentences or checking how a name is spelt when you are writing – just write.

Once you have finished your draft and are ready to start editing, you become a different person. Just as you closed off your editor's mind while you were writing, you now become an editor by putting away the writer side of you. You view your book as objectively as you can and approach it in a purely practical way.

Having this division is how I get the best results in both writing and editing.

Editing your book can seem like a huge mountain to climb, but it doesn't need to be. Even if you decide to engage the services of an editor, I still believe it's a huge asset to be able to edit your books yourself. It will save you money handing over a polished manuscript to an editor, because they won't need to spend so much time on it. Or if you choose to completely self-edit, you can use these editing steps to go through your manuscript again and again, smoothing it out each time.

I was very fortunate in the beginning to have one of my lovely blog readers Rose offer to edit my book *Thirty Chic Days*. When I asked her why she was volunteering her time, she told me she believed in my work and also enjoyed my blog writing, so I suppose it was fun for her as well as being helpful for me.

Rose had a background editing government publications in her home country of Australia, so felt confident she would do a good job. Now that I am a bit further down the track in my writing career, I can see how it would be a fun and satisfying thing to do – to help a new writer whose work you enjoyed reading.

Seeing how she tweaked sentences and offered suggestions taught me a lot, and I am very grateful for her effort and expertise. At the time I sent her gifts and gift vouchers even though she hadn't asked for payment. I never got to meet her – we emailed chapters back and forth, and sadly she died from breast cancer; so early, she was only in her sixties.

I am grateful Rose reached out to me and offered her help, and I feel glad that I accepted it too.

The only other time I have used an editor is one I employed through Fiverr.com. It was expensive-ish – several hundred dollars (although I know others can spend thousands on editing) but unfortunately, I didn't feel like I received good value for money. She seemed to have made a lot of changes, but when I sat down and went through them all, they were quite basic (such as changing a time description from '6am' to '6.00 a.m.').

I also picked up errors in subsequent read-throughs that she hadn't (many of which were quite obvious), when her reviews said how amazing she was and had picked up deliberately planted errors. Well she didn't pick up mine! But still, you live and learn.

Because of this experience I am more than happy to continue on editing my own books, because I know the more I do it, the more I'll learn, and the better I will get – hopefully! In addition, it's *my* voice that comes through, because with every person who changes your words, your writing style will be skewed away from you ever so slightly.

After editing a few of my books I started putting together the steps, because it is a process you go through, and I wanted to note down everything that worked well for my editing; that way I wouldn't forget a vital step.

My Successful Author editing checklist:

1. Spellcheck.
2. Read in head.
3. Read out loud to myself.
4. Add chapter numbers once the order is finalized.
5. Add sub-headings into each chapter.
6. Check words that are habitually overused without me realizing – 'really', 'just', etc.
7. Remove as many apostrophes as possible.
8. Spellcheck.

Spell check

I always start off my editing process with a spell-check on the computer. This corrects obvious errors quickly, which means I'm not snagged by them as I go through the editing process. Even though I mostly pick up errors as I go, there will be some that I have missed.

My mum laughed once when I told her I don't do a spellcheck in emails, because I'm a good speller and I don't get words wrong. She liked my confidence! Of course, since then she takes delight in pointing out any errors I might let slip through, and I give her the same courtesy.

I remember my mum when I am tempted to skip yet another spell check on my work. I'd hate an unnecessary typo to be published in one of my books.

Read in your head

The next step after spell check is to read your book. If you want to print it, please do. Reading from paper can make a difference to your comprehension. I printed out *Thirty Chic Days* and read it that way, but with other books I've read them from the screen.

As you read, check that you have your point of view consistent. You don't want to change from first person to third person in the same sentence for example.

I also send my book document to my Kindle and read it that way. If you have a Kindle or Kindle app, there is an email address you can send documents to, so you can create your own Kindle books. To find out your Kindle email address, simply go to this Amazon help page:

https://www.amazon.com/gp/help/customer/display.html?nodeId=201974220

Or search for 'how to find out your kindle email address'.

Reading the book on a Kindle gives you a slightly different reading experience, much like reading on paper versus a screen.

Basically, you will want to read the same manuscript in different ways to ensure you pick up as many improvement opportunities as possible.

I read the book right through in the normal manner, and I have also found it helpful to read backwards too: chapter by chapter starting at the end. This is especially good if you can't face reading your book *one more time*, even though you know you must. Starting with the last chapter brings about a freshness which is welcomed.

Read out loud

Reading your work out loud is *the* best tip I can offer. It makes a huge difference which you will find out once you do it. Awkwardly worded areas stand out, and it's incredible the difference switching a few words around can make to a sentence flowing smoother. Some sentences read fine on the page, but once they are said out loud sound totally different.

See if there are any sentences you can simplify or shorten too. Try to make your ideas as clear as possible. If you have a paragraph you are not happy with but can't easily see how to make it better, consider rewriting it. Start typing underneath it and explain the concept differently. Then, delete the original paragraph.

Don't be afraid to move paragraphs around either. Sometimes I'll explain one idea and move naturally onto the next one. Then I'll drift back to the first idea thus repeating myself somewhat. So, I'll merge those two parts of the first idea together and it reads much better.

Add chapter numbers and headings

Once you have finalized the order of your chapters, add in chapter numbers, and headings, if applicable.

If you already have chapter titles, see if they could be catchier or match the content of that chapter better. This is something I've had to learn to do. I'd be very happy with chapter titles that plainly describe what the chapter is about, but I know that the eye is caught by 'sexier' titles.

For example, the wardrobe chapter in *Thirty Chic Days* could easily have been named simply 'Your Closet', but instead I titled it, 'Curate your wardrobe like it is your own bijou boutique' which is far more interesting. This is the chapter version of judging a book by its cover. If you start reading a chapter which has an exciting title, you are set up to enjoy it far more than a chapter which has a somewhat perfunctory heading.

Add sub-headings into each chapter

As with enticing chapter names, I'd be quite content to leave my chapters as a big block of text (it's called 'laziness'), but I know that they will be easier and more enjoyable to read with sub-headings, so I add those in too.

Read through the chapter and identify natural 'breaks' where one topic flows to the next. Summarize each area with a sub-heading.

A regular criticism I have seen of self-published books is that topics written about are not well organized, meander all over the place, or are disjointed.

Creating sub-headings in your chapters is an excellent way to avoid this, and it helps you organize your thoughts better too. If you are working from an outline you will probably already have sub-headings in place, but if your outline only includes chapter ideas, you will want to add in sub-headings.

There is no right or wrong way, I've done both, but unless your chapters are very short, say if you wrote a '101 ways to do X'-type book with short and punchy chapters, sub-headings will likely be necessary.

Search for weak, overused and lazy words

Choosing a spelling and grammar check rather than only a spell check will start you off with this, and you would be wise to continue searching for weak, overused and lazy words.

There will be words you overuse without realizing; a mix of 'lazy' words that slip into many people's writing, and your own words that crop up a lot. After this refining step, your writing will be tightened up which makes it more pleasing and easier to absorb for the reader.

You will want to hunt out those words and delete or replace them with other words. I put together my own list which I have added to over time, and when I am editing a book, I do a word-search and consider the merits of each of these words as I find them. I ask myself questions such as:

Is this word necessary? (sometimes they can be deleted without affecting the sentence e.g. 'just'.)

Could I use a better word? (some words are weak and dull e.g. 'thing' when you could use a more descriptive word.)

Do I use this word a lot or is it used twice in one paragraph? (research alternatives in a thesaurus or from your own mind.)

Here is a list of words I 'weed out' as much as possible, and I find it makes my writing more interesting, plus it flows better. You'll see after you have done this that your writing is elevated to a new level.

Is
Was
Had
Has
Could
Are
That
Just
And
Some
Really
Very
Sometimes
Then
Stuff
Things
Got
Was/Is/Are/Am
Went

Search for one word at a time and evaluate each instance in which they are used. Can you delete or change the word? Or are you happy to leave it as is?

The words above will inevitably crop up when I am writing, but I don't do anything about them at the time.

I know I can sort them out later and not interrupt my creative flow.

Weak words

Saying 'I believe…' (or 'I think…') or 'it's my opinion that…' in a book is weak apparently. When my editor friend Rose went through my first draft, she crossed out all the examples of 'I believe' and 'It's my opinion that'. She also said I shouldn't be so apologetic in my writing: in other words, to own what I was saying.

An example of this could be:
I believe that we all have the right to earn a good living.

Rose crossed out the first three words:
~~*I believe that*~~ *We all have the right to earn a good living.*

At first I wondered if I could own that statement, but then saw that people would already know it was what I believed, and could choose to agree or disagree. It's the same with your opinion; it's just different ways of wording things, so cross those out too:

It's my opinion that financial skills should be taught in high school.

~~It's my opinion that~~ *Financial skills should be taught in high school.*

See how the edited sentences come across much stronger? This is still a step I struggle with – owning statements like this can be hard! – but I try to remember what Rose taught me and delete those phrases.

Look at all apostrophes

As much as possible I change words such as you'd, I'd, I'll etc, into full words e.g. *you'll* into *you will*. What I have found is that as I type in flow, I'll write in a more informal way.

I change a lot of apostrophe examples to the full two words, but not all of them. When I am reading through my work, I can see which ones should stay. It's more an art than a science.

I like to leave some in because they make my writing easy to read and more relatable. Taking every apostrophe out makes the book too formal and stuffy, but taking some of them out stops it being too informal.

How many you leave in will be dictated by your own writing 'voice', which appears naturally when you type how you talk.

Using a thesaurus

When I am doing my editing, I find online tools such as thesaurus.com and dictionary websites extremely helpful. For instance, I might have used the same word 'lovely' twice in one sentence or paragraph. I will notice that it doesn't look right to have repeated a word so closely, so I brainstorm possible alternatives for one of the instances (or both, if the word is one that I habitually overuse, which 'lovely' can be.)

If I draw a blank or am not in the most creative mood, I'll check thesaurus.com. Putting in that word will bring up other possibilities. I try a few and then carry on once I am satisfied. I have found doing this has expanded my vocabulary (or at least my writing vocabulary) which is great.

Seeing all those alternatives also gets me excited at the unlimitedness of words and writing, and I am fired up all over again!

Final spell check

Then, once you have gone through the other points in the editing steps list, do a final spellcheck at the end to set your mind at ease. When you are making small corrections during the editing steps, wrongly spelled words or missing letters may crop up. That's why I don't rely on the first spellcheck only.

Along the same lines, check the spelling of any websites and names you have used too, even if you are fairly confident they are all correct.

When I re-published *A Chic and Simple Christmas* with the new cover, I re-read the manuscript and also added a few new pieces to the content. At the very last minute when I was going through names used in the book, I saw that I had written 'Megan Markle' instead of 'Meghan Markle'. It wouldn't have been the end of the world, but I often judge writers if I see they have gotten a person's name wrong and I don't want to be *that* author!

Successful author action tips:

Don't try to rush or skip any steps in the editing process. I know how exciting it is to publish your book, but it will be for sale for a long time so you want to do a good job. Even if you decide to go through it again at a later date, there will be people who have ordered your book before that and they will have the first copy forever. If it's lazily edited it will reflect poorly on you and it may put them off ordering any of your future books.

Take your time with editing, without procrastinating too much or being a perfectionist about it. It's a balance between doing a good job and not letting it take forever.

I have found the occasional error in traditionally published books from major authors, so it's something that's going to happen. Of course you will want to do everything you can to sift them out, but don't let the fear of errors be something that prevents you from publishing.

Chapter 14
Creating a beautiful cover for your book

I'm not sure who first said, 'Don't judge a book by its cover', but I don't think it's very good advice. An attractive cover on a book makes it far more appealing to me, and I know I can't be the only one. An enticing cover gives me a good feeling before I've even read a word, which means I am going in with a more positive state of mind. This can only mean good things, right?

And likewise, if a book has a dreary or boring cover, I have to almost drag myself to read it, even if the subject or premise appeals. I'm sure that dull cover affects how much I enjoy the book too.

Aside from how your book reflects the contents and affects the reader's experience, you also want to stand out amongst all those other books which are for sale in the marketplace, whether it's on a website or bookstore shelf. So it's in your best interest to have a cover which catches the reader's eye and makes them want to know more.

You will be pleased to know that covers don't need to cost a fortune either.

When I first started self-publishing five years ago, I did everything myself at no cost. I wanted to see if I could make money from my writing and not spend it all on expensive services. I wanted my writing to become my job and my income, not a pricy hobby.

Free and low-cost book covers

My first covers were designed with the free cover creator service within Amazon's self-publishing service Kindle Direct Publishing (or KDP for short). They offer a small range of free images and cover designs. You can further customize your cover with colour. These covers did a great job for me starting out, and it didn't take me too long to put them together either. And, they were the right price at the time – free.

My next step was to invest USD$10 for a cover image. Believe me, at the time this was a huge step. I bought the image from Canva.com, which is a fantastic website to play around with (I still use their free version today).

They have free images too, but not as much of a selection as if you pay. As well, there are other websites such as Unsplash.com who offer royalty-free images. Before you publish a book, pay careful attention to the terms surrounding the image you choose, because you don't want to get into trouble.

I used that $10 Canva image within the same KDP free cover creator service. By purchasing an image, I had a much greater choice, plus there was less chance of seeing another book with my cover image on it.

You might have noticed when browsing Amazon's Kindle books that some covers have similarities to other authors covers. When you go to design your cover in KDP you will see why – they look exactly like the templates.

But you don't have to look the same as everyone else, even with the free cover creator service. Just have a play around and mock up some covers to see what feels most like you and your writing topic. Imagine you are the reader browsing Amazon to purchase as you design your cover.

Finding your ideal image style

Those free and low-cost covers worked perfectly for me for years, and I used them well into being completely self-employed, having replaced my job income. I wanted to share this to show that it is possible. You don't have to spend a fortune to do well.

When I came to publish my book *Thirty More Chic Days* though, I wanted to try a new kind of cover style;

one that looked a little more professional and like a 'real' book. I was very grateful to my old covers at how far they'd brought me, and I was excited to upgrade to something new.

I desired a more customized experience and to take my book covers to the next level. Initially I planned to hire an illustrator to create bespoke images that I would own, and be the only person who could use them.

I made contact with a few artists on Etsy and also sent emails to websites I researched. I found these names by browsing book covers in my genre and taking a 'Look Inside' with the Amazon function to see if the illustrator was mentioned. I found a couple of names that way. However, some artists never bothered responding, and the few who did said they were too busy.

This was a little disheartening, but I continued on with my quest. I started looking at stock image websites which I found by searching for 'stock photos' and going with the ones that came up most often.

On these stock image websites, I found lovely 'fashion and style' line drawings that I imagined could be on my covers. Yes, in theory anyone could also put them on *their* book cover, so mine wouldn't be unique, but I saw that there were thousands upon thousands of illustrations and decided the risk was extremely low that someone would choose the same illustration in the same genre as me.

Sometimes I would find an image I liked but saw that the illustrator had done only one or two of its type, or there weren't similar illustrations from other artists. This was important to me because I had several covers I wanted to update, and also plan to write many more books. I wanted to find an artist that not only did I love their look and which I felt encompassed the feeling I wanted for my books (aspirational, stylish and elegant, at the same time as being welcoming and friendly), but who also had many options to enable me to build a cohesive 'brand look'.

The artist I have gone with has a lot of images ('Marisa_' on depositphotos.com). Some aren't 'me', but there are plenty which are, and I know I will have fun choosing an illustration from her catalogue for each new book cover.

It took me quite a while to find my illustrator and the images I went with, but it was worth the digging through many pages on stock image sites because now it's easy – I just search that one artist's images. You will probably find you also have to put the time in and find images and an illustrator who projects the feeling you want to portray with your books.

I saved every image that I thought could be a possible contender into a file on my computer (you are allowed to do this, you just aren't allowed to use them, and they have a watermark over the image until you purchase) and let them sit for a few days. It helped to quickly mock up some covers on Canva too, so I could see them in context and imagine if they were 'me'.

I even went so far as trying to purchase some but got bogged down by all the options: buy 1, buy 10, monthly subscription. Gosh, which was the better deal and would I use them all?

And, I still needed to find someone to design the cover or learn to do it myself. Creating covers sounded fun, but I also knew that it would take a lot of time away from my actual writing to learn how to do it well. I felt it was better to outsource to a professional who would do a much better job, and for me to get back to my writing. You might be different; perhaps you are a whizz in graphic design, but I am not.

Hiring a graphic designer

After my disappointing experience with custom illustrators, I had the idea to look at freelance graphic designers on Fiverr.com and came across a lady called Les who goes by the handle 'germancreative'. For USD$15 she would create a Kindle and print copy cover, plus a 3D image of the book which you can use for marketing. The price also includes the cost of one or two stock images.

I tried her for the first of my new covers when publishing *Thirty More Chic Days*, and *loved it*. For not much more than purchasing the rights to use those same images myself, my graphic designer created the entire cover, including the type of font I wanted, as well as making both eBook and print covers for me (which need to be 'wrap-around': back cover, spine and front cover.)

I don't have a graphic design program and am not a graphic designer, so it would have taken me *an age* to create my own cover and it wouldn't have looked as good either. As I said, I would much rather outsource this job to someone else and get on with my writing (or editing as the case usually is when I get to the point where I am ready to have my cover made.)

Once *Thirty More Chic Days* was out, I started updating my other books with new covers too, sending Les a new job every couple of weeks. I now have an illustrator I love, and I have fun choosing font colours to harmonize with the image on each cover. This made the covers quick to put together and it was all because I took the time to ensure I got my first new cover right. After that, it was simple to replicate for other books.

I love the look of all my new covers and yes, they really do feel like 'me'. Take your time and enjoy the process of putting your look together, because your covers are an important part of your book. Plus, it's fun to see your 'brand' evolve. The exciting feeling you get from your covers is the same feeling your readers will, so be enthusiastic, and fall in love with your covers.

Successful author action tips:

Starting out

When you are just beginning to self-publish, doing something such as contracting a graphic designer may seem quite 'big'; I know it would have to me. I wanted to keep things simple and use the no-cost/low-cost/non-scary options first. That's why I went with KDP's free cover creator that you will come across when you are uploading your book.

If I was starting out again, I'd probably try a few free covers, and once I'd broken the psychological barrier of publishing, I think I'd go straight to my Fiverr covers. They aren't that expensive and to me they look far more professional and like 'real books' than my earlier covers.

See what feels best for you. If you are happy to spend the money and want to jump straight in, hire a graphic designer. Or, you might be a whizz at graphic design, so why not give it a go yourself?

And, if you're a nervous wee thing like I was in the beginning, go and have a play around in KDP's free cover creator service. You can always change your covers later if you want to.

Research covers in your genre, or that you love the look of

Browse through Amazon for books similar to yours and see what the covers look like. Save images and links of those which appeal. Then when you come to make a cover or hire a graphic designer, you will already have ideas and inspiration to be guided by.

Also, look on your bookshelves at home. Likely you will enjoy reading books in the same genre you are writing in, so take inspiration from those books as well.

Look at the covers and pick out what appeals. Is it the colours used? Photograph versus illustration? The font? Make notes of what you like and then you'll have guidelines for your own fabulous covers.

Mocking up a cover as a motivator

I have heard the advice to have your cover made first to spur you on. You are acting as if the book already exists, so it makes it easier to complete because the book seems real in your mind – *but* the problem I came across is an entirely practical roadblock to this idea and it's this: if you are publishing in print as well, you have to provide the page count to your cover designer (because the spine size will vary) and I never know the final page count until I've finished the book.

However, if you are writing a book for Kindle only (which my graphic designer only charges US$5 a cover for), you can totally do this. All you have to do in this case is have decided on your title and subtitle and chosen an image. Imagine having that book cover as your screen saver; how motivating would that be?

If you feel like the advance cover method might give you a boost but want to make things less scary, there is nothing to stop you from going into Canva.com and mocking up a free cover. I have done this and it's a good interim step. Canva has plenty of Kindle cover templates, and who knows, you might even find one to publish on your real Kindle book for free.

Create your back-cover blurb

If you are doing a print copy of your book, you will need to come up with a back-cover blurb. I usually use parts of my introduction – three paragraphs in total is a good length – so I'll copy and paste sections I think will describe the book well, and refine from there.

That same piece can then be used as your book description when uploading your manuscript to Amazon.

Chapter 15
Formatting your book for publication

Your first question when it comes to publishing time is whether you should do Kindle or paperback, or both. Print copies require more work than eBooks. There is the formatting, so it looks like an enticing book to read, extra work needed for the cover, and rather importantly, making sure all the page numbers match the table of contents.

If you want to make it an easier on yourself, start with just Kindle in the beginning. With my books, I have consistently found that more than three-quarters of sales are Kindle, and only a quarter are paperback. Sometimes it skews even higher, to 85% Kindle and 15% paperback.

I started out only offering Kindle books, then, after a while once I got my confidence up, I started publishing in paperback as well.

Publishing a Kindle book is *so easy*: as easy as uploading a Word document to a website. If you know how to send an email, you can publish a Kindle book. Basically, you write your book, add page breaks between chapters or sections and you're done.

Why I publish in print

You can certainly skip this part and go straight to the 'Publishing on Kindle' section. Do this if it means an easier start to publishing your first (or next) book. But why not do print as well at some stage? You will reach more readers, you will be able to be stocked in libraries and bookstores, and having a print copy somehow makes your book feel more 'legit'.

In addition, there are many who prefer to read on paper and some people don't own a Kindle, iPad or any such device to download a Kindle book. Anyone can download the Kindle app to their desktop or laptop, but it's not the most fun thing to read a whole book sitting at your computer.

It's fabulous to order a few copies of your own book to have on the bookshelf at home too. Who wouldn't want to see that?

It's funny, when I place an 'author copy' order for my books, I generally purchase five or ten of a title. And, they invariably all disappear. Some readers who live in New Zealand or Australia ask to order a print copy from me rather than have it sent from the United States. They are great to do a giveaway for readers of your blog or social media. And you can send a review copy to a fellow author or blogger for publicity.

I also have friends and neighbours occasionally 'borrow' one of my titles to read. I don't mind if they are never returned; hopefully they are still doing the rounds!

How to format your print version first

For the publishing process, I start with the print version and do the necessary formatting, and then once it's finished and uploaded, I strip out all the formatting and extra page breaks, make the headings slightly smaller and upload the simplified version to KDP as a Kindle copy.

The reason I do it this way is that when I am producing the print version to look like a real book interior, I find parts I want to change, correct, make better and add to.

When I started off the other way around – doing the Kindle version first then formatting into a paperback file, I ended up having to go back and change the Kindle version too. It was double-handling at best, and having two different copies of the same book at worst (if I missed going back and correcting something).

It's far easier to catch everything when starting with the formatted print version I've found, so I stick to formatting in that order.

With my first book that was published in print, I downloaded a template from KDP and used that. It was very helpful and the only major change I made was changing the font to one I found easier to read. The default font on the template was 'Garamond' which, on paper, was quite light in colour, so I changed to my favourite 'Georgia' font, with 'High Tower Text' for chapter titles.

Then, with subsequent books I used the same template and fonts, which means I have a continuity to how my books look and read.

You can search for 'Paperback Manuscript Templates' under the KDP Help area (or search for 'kdp help paperback manuscript templates' and it should be the first option to come up).

I used the 'Templates with sample content' because I found the chapter headings, page and section breaks, etc. very useful. Click on 'Templates with sample content' and you will see a list of book sizes available.

The sizes I chose for my book templates were based on books on my shelves at home and seeing what I liked the look of. In the end I chose 5.5" x 8.5" for my larger/longer books and 5" x 8" for my smaller/shorter books.

For my larger books I use 12pt size 'Georgia' for the body of the text, and 20pt size 'High Tower Text' for chapter headings and other main titles. For my smaller books I make the 'Georgia' font slightly smaller to 11pt size (keeping my titles the same 20pt size 'High Tower Text'). I originally used 12pt size 'Georgia' for both book sizes, but in the smaller book the text looked like Large Print, so I scaled it back to 11pt. One of my pet peeves is books with teeny tiny font (and I have pretty good eyesight) but I had gone too far the other way!

Why not download a template straight away and have a play around? You can even start typing directly into the template and feel like you are writing a 'real book'– because you are.

The benefits of starting with a blank page

For me it feels more freeing to start typing a new chapter into a fresh Word document, then I don't have to feel constricted by keeping to the formatted areas. I don't want anything to cramp my style or interrupt my flow.

I type each chapter into a separate Word document, so I can easily see how many words that chapter has. Once I have finished the chapters I start moving them over into the template. There is a little bit of reformatting to get it looking like the template did to start with, but I find this less of a problem than feeling like my creativity keeps getting interfered with, or not knowing how long a chapter is.

You may not be bothered by either of these things and find redoing the formatting more of a pain, so may prefer to type your book directly into the template. There are no rights, wrongs or rules; just give everything a go and see which you prefer.

The template already contains page breaks and section breaks, and I also add in page breaks as necessary, so that the look of the page is pleasing. For example, if a chapter subtitle is on one page but the corresponding text starts on the next, I will insert a page break at the end of the previous body of text. This serves to drop the sub-heading to the next page, where it looks better because the title and section are kept together.

Again, do research with books you already own, especially similar types of books – for example, I would look at non-fiction books in a similar size to mine (and with no pictures, because I don't use pictures) to get ideas for how I want mine to look.

I chose to justify my paragraphs (which means the left and right sides of the text are straight down) and also increase the line spacing slightly. To me it just looks better, and my eye finds it easier to read. I played around and liked 1.2 line spacing, then made it 1.21, which is my personal quirk embedded into all of my books. My birthday falls on the 21st of October, so 21 is 'my' number. You don't have to make your line spacing the same as your birthday, of course, but you can if you want to!

How to create your table of contents

As you start adding your written chapters into the formatted template, you will want to create a table of contents, to be able to move around the document quickly and easily, and also because you will need it for the finished product. I have described how to create one in *Chapter 6*, but I will do a recap here as well.

In my Microsoft program it's the first section under 'References' along the top banner of my screen.

Click on 'Table of Contents' to insert a table (there isn't much difference between any of the options that I can see, so choose whichever one you like), then start scrolling through to your chapter titles. Highlight each one in turn, choosing Level 1 under 'Add Text'. Optional: do the same with sub-headings which will be Level 2 and so forth.

The cool thing about creating a table of contents (which I always do as soon as I collate all my chapters into one document) is that it gives you a real-time guide of your book's chapters down the left-hand side of your screen in the Navigation pane.

Make sure you update your table of contents as you go (right click, 'Update Field'), so that your chapter headings and page numbers match the content. This is particularly important at the very end to ensure your print copy shows correct information in the table of contents.

If you need more detailed instructions or your program is different to mine, simply search for 'how to create a table of contents in X' (insert your computer detail whether it is Apple Mac or Microsoft etc) and you'll find helpful websites with images. Tech people love creating useful blog posts for any niche topic, which is wonderful.

Authors are just as generous. Whenever I've been stuck over some little point in my self-publishing journey, I simply search for the question and have found many helpful self-publishing blogs and websites. No matter what you can't work out, there will have been someone who has had the same issue and shares how they have overcome it. Often it's just a tiny tweak.

Saving your work as a print-ready file

Once you are happy with how your formatted book looks and reads, you will need to save it as a PDF file to upload to KDP for your print copy. Don't use the 'File, Save as PDF' option though. There is a preferable way to produce a PDF file and it is called 'Print to PDF'.

Apparently, this embeds fonts or whatever needs to be done so that things don't move around when your manuscript begins its process of being converted to a paperback book by KDP. I don't know all the technical details of how this works, but I do know that before I used this type of PDF conversion, sometimes a few words would slip onto the next page when I uploaded my print copy to KDP and it would throw the page count out. This was very frustrating, so I was so glad to find out about 'Print to PDF'. It sticks everything in place and keeps it there.

Proceed as if you were going to print out the pages in the normal way (File, Print...), but instead of using your default printer, choose 'Print to PDF'. It should take a few seconds to run through the pages and then prompt you to save the file. Make it clear when you name it that this is the file you will be uploading to KDP, so there is no room for confusion!

The importance of Print Preview

When your manuscript and cover are uploaded to KDP, it's time to use the Print Previewer. By all means go ahead and order a physical proof copy to be sent to you if you want. I did for my first couple of titles, but after that I trusted they would look just like the online Print Previewer, and they did.

Don't be tempted to skip the Print Preview though, and do be prepared to go through the entire book several times. The kinds of things I look out for are accidentally empty pages, and the 'shape' of the text so that the look of the pages are pleasing. Even errors can be picked up as you flick through from page to page (they seem to catch the eye.)

It's a bit of a bother when I pick up something to correct, as it means going back to the Word document, making the change, printing to PDF, uploading to KDP and starting the online Print Previewer all over again.

The only thing that stops me from thinking, 'Oh I don't need to go through the 300 pages again, they were fine last time', is that once I submit the book, it will be up on Amazon *forever*, with people paying for it; so I feel it's my duty and honour as a writer to make it as good as I can.

When you are doing the final edits and uploading the manuscript, it's a balance between doing a good job and feeling proud that you've done your best, without being a procrastinating perfectionist. Just keep at it until you can happily approve that final Print Preview, and pat yourself on the back for a job well done.

Your print copy will generally be approved in the next 24-48 hours, and in the meantime you can get on with uploading your Kindle version (which doesn't take as long as the print copy to go live once you've submitted it.)

Publishing on Kindle

Here is the process I use to adjust the print copy version to make it better suited for reading on a Kindle or other device. Firstly, I make a 'File, Save As' copy of the document so I end up with two separate documents for Print and Kindle.

Then, on the new Kindle document, I go through and change all the 20pt size headings to 16pt size. 20 is just too big to look good on Kindle in my experience.

I take out all the extra page breaks which were necessary in the print copy. I leave in only one page break at the end of each chapter, so that every new chapter (and extras such as Contents, About the Author etc.) starts on a new Kindle 'page'.

I leave the line spacing at 1.21; that's still fine for Kindle. In fact, I prefer it for books I read on Kindle. Those that are published in single line spacing are quite squashed looking to me and require more concentration, whereas line spacing that is a little more spread out is easier to read.

I also simplify the beginning of the book – the title, copyright etc. In the print copy the title and subtitle on the first page is huge, but on the Kindle copy I take it right down to 16pt size. The copyright information remains the same 10pt size in Calibri font in both.

I then remove the ISBN code, because this is only required for the print version (I use the free ISBN code provided by KDP). Lastly I remove the page break under the main title bringing the copyright information to sit right under the title of the book. The first two print copy pages are merged into one in the Kindle version.

Following is an example from my book *Thirty More Chic Days*; firstly the print copy (first two pages):

(first page)

THIRTY MORE CHIC DAYS

Creating an inspired mindset for a magical life

FIONA FERRIS

THE CHIC AUTHOR

(at the bottom of the second page)

Copyright © 2018 Fiona Ferris

All rights reserved.

ISBN: 9781723722899

Then, the Kindle copy (both pages combined):

THIRTY MORE CHIC DAYS

Creating an inspired mindset for a magical life

FIONA FERRIS

howtobechic.com
fionaferris.com

Copyright © 2018 Fiona Ferris
All rights reserved.

If you are reading this book on Kindle, I apologize for just how big the print copy text is, but it demonstrates perfectly why I change it!

The final touch is to add links, or make links live, so readers can click through directly to a website from the Kindle edition. I add my websites in between the title and copyright information, as you can see above.

I also make links live in my 'Other books by Fiona Ferris' (to each of my titles on Amazon), 'About the Author' (to each of my social media URLs) and 'Book Bonuses' (the link to my email list signup).

And that's all I really change for my Kindle version. It's nice and easy. You don't even need to change the format of your file once you've finished; the recommended file type to use is Word, which is what you're using to type in.

Then, it's a matter of uploading your Word file manuscript and Kindle cover to KDP as with the print version, and committing to as many Print Previews as you need before you submit your book.

The most common thing I find when previewing one of my Kindle eBooks online is that I've missed deleting a page break from the print version in the middle of a chapter, so I'll go back, take it out, upload the document and preview again.

Successful author action tip:

Make it easy to get your first book out

If the thought of formatting a paperback fills you with dread, leave your print copy aside to do later, or not at all. Make things nice and easy for yourself, and have a go at uploading a simple Word document to KDP.

Then, once your Kindle copy is live you might decide to have a play around creating a print copy. Or you might not, and be happy with having your books available as eBooks only. Loads of authors do this.

Chapter 16
Self-publishing or traditional publishing?

Now that you've finished your book, how do you get it to your readers? That was the very question which stopped me even contemplating writing my first book for a long time. As I have mentioned, I live in New Zealand, population: nearly five million, at the bottom of the world. There aren't enough people here to buy more than a few copies of my book, plus, how do I get it to them?

And I couldn't even fathom how to get my book to people in other countries. It all just seemed too big and too hard, so it was easier just to keep my writing dream... a dream. But thanks to all the advances in technology now, we live in a global marketplace and our opportunities are much expanded.

In the old days of traditional publishing, you were either accepted by the publisher or you weren't. You didn't have much choice in the matter aside from putting yourself up for consideration in the first place. The publisher had to decide if they could make money from you or not, because after all, they are running a business.

Traditional publishing is certainly still there, but it's not as easy for the publisher anymore. Despite this, many people think that what they see in a bookshop is all there is. In fact, this selection is just the tip of the iceberg of what's available. People I talk to in my real life can't see how I can have written and published several books and sold forty thousand copies, yet they're not able to go down the road and buy them.

I have considered visiting local bookstores and showing them copies of my books to see if they'd like to order them in, but the more I considered it, the less keen I was. Firstly, it would be excruciating, especially for an introvert such as myself. 'Please buy my book?' I'd whimper. And then their response, 'What sort of rubbish is this? Chic? What?' they'd be saying to me.

And it would be more of a vanity measure than anything else, because they would likely only sell a handful of books in a year, whereas currently online dozens every day are purchased by my readers, sometimes hundreds a day when I release a new book or have publicity such as an interview.

Being online gives you a world-wide audience without having to ask someone face-to-face to put their faith in your writing. The audience can decide for themselves from the book sample, and by reading reviews. Plus, they might already know that they like your writing style and what you talk about, if they follow your blog or social media.

When you are deciding between self-publishing and traditional publishing, there certainly are pros and cons to both. Here are some of those as I see them:

Traditional publishing

Pros

- Has more of a cachet (although self-publishing has become more mainstream these days.)
- You may gain a wider audience.
- If you really hit it big, you could become quite famous.
- You receive an advance royalty payment up front.

Cons

- You receive low royalties compared with self-publishing – for eBooks you might receive 15% royalty versus 35%-70% with self-publishing.

- You still have to do quite a lot of your own marketing; the publisher doesn't do everything for you while you sit back relaxing with a cocktail by the pool.
- Royalties beyond your advance can take years to materialize.
- The publishing house chooses how your book will look, and what goes on the cover.

Self-publishing

Pros

- You have complete control over your work and can write what you want, as well as have the cover looking exactly how you want.
- You receive far higher royalties and are paid within sixty days.
- It's easier to be niche, and thanks to the Internet your readers will find you (you can help them out too, with your marketing.)

Cons

- You have to do all the work yourself, or find someone to outsource it to – editing, formatting, cover design, uploading, marketing etc

I know of a self-published author who earns a lot – one monthly payment she mentioned was $70,000 – yes really, and in a single month! I heard from one of her friends that she turned down a traditional publishing deal because it would have meant her receiving a big drop in income, and for what reason? If she was already earning an amazing income each month, why would she want to give that up?

Some want to be traditionally published for the prestige of being accepted by a well-known name in the book world, and some have a desire to be famous and use their books to springboard their way into bigger things, such as a television show, or international recognition and fame.

Be the exact kind of author you want to be

It just depends what you want, and what suits your personality and lifestyle. For me, I don't desire fame and I just want to create my own income working from home. My dream is to be 'a housewife who writes books'. When I was getting myself all wound up thinking, 'I should be doing more, I'm too lazy, I'm not putting enough into my writing and marketing', I calmed myself down by asking what I really wanted. The answer I came up with is that I wanted to be a housewife who wrote books. I wanted to live a beautiful, peaceful and relaxing life at home, while writing.

Being an author isn't the biggest part of my life, *my life* is. But still, it's my job too. A fantastic job where I work as many hours as I wish from the comfort of my home office, with pets napping in their bed under my desk. It's fantastic.

And that is why I choose to self-publish. I'm not letting anyone else down if my book isn't finished by a certain date. If I have something unexpected crop up I can 'take a day off'.

Recently my husband (who works in car sales) had to deliver a car to a customer in a city about four hours drive away. He said he'd really like me to come and I could look around the shops and have lunch while he was talking to the lady about her new car, then we'd both drive home in her old car in the afternoon. I love that I can do things like this without going to a boss and asking for the day off.

'I am a housewife who writes books'. It suits me perfectly.

Maybe you're different. Maybe you want to take over the world with your books and your message, becoming super-famous in the process. It's all your choice!

Great things can happen when you self-publish

So there I was, happily going along writing my books and self-publishing them on Amazon, when I received a strange email in my Inbox. It was three Christmases ago because I remember I received it at Christmas time. The email was from a lady in Lithuania saying that her company wanted to publish my book *Thirty Chic Days* in Lithuanian. She asked me to send her a digital copy of the book by return email.

I froze! Was she a spammer? A hacker? Someone who looked legitimate but would turn around and sell my book on the black market? Change the name and publish it herself?

After a few back and forth emails I found out that she was real, and her employer was the oldest publishing house in Lithuania. Simple and quick online searches showed that I could trust her, so I sent a PDF copy of *Thirty Chic Days* and hoped for the best (praying that I hadn't just walked into the hands of an unscrupulous person!)

Eventually I received the contract from her company, signed it and sent it back to Lithuania and they then had their translator re-write my book in their language. I received my advance payment up front and many months later my book was published in Lithuanian. I have copies of it on my bookshelf right now. I can't read a word on any page, but I know exactly what the book says.

And later on, the same thing happened with a Russian publisher (I have just signed a contract to have them translate a second book of mine, *Thirty Slim Days*, in Russian as well), and a Vietnamese publisher. *They all approached me, I didn't pitch them.* As I said in *Chapter 1*, incredible things like this happen when you put yourself out there.

I feel like I have the best of both worlds with traditional publishing vs. self-publishing, because I have my English books self-published on Amazon, and three foreign languages through traditional publishing houses. I would never have translated my books into other languages. So to me, the small advance I received and the possibility of ongoing royalties is free money that I wouldn't have had otherwise.

Plus, how cool is it to have books published in other languages? I get a thrill every time I go past my bookcase and see the foreign copies of my books. Plus, receiving happy messages from my Lithuanian and Russian readers is fabulous (my Vietnamese translation is still in progress).

I have 'met' the loveliest ladies who excitedly tell me how they have gained so much from reading my books (thank goodness for translation capabilities on social media and free online translation services such as Google Translate!)

Successful author action tips:

Relax, you're covered

Don't worry about making a decision whether you want to self-publish or approach a publishing house just now. Just know that if you write a book, it will be published one way or the other. There's no need to let uncertainty stop you from writing.

You can search for a publisher *and* self-publish at the same time if you want. Many successful authors who have contracts with big publishing houses started out by self-publishing. EL James of *Fifty Shades of Grey* fame did. No matter what you think of her subject matter you can't deny she has made it big.

If you hanker after being a traditionally published author, give yourself the best odds of being discovered and put your work out there.

Work out what kind of author you want to be

Do you desire fame and fortune? Or just a more creative life where you call the shots? Would you like to go on a big book tour or does that thought make you break out in a cold sweat, because you are shy and feel happier writing from behind the scenes?

You can be any type of author you like; there is room for everyone. The exciting thing about starting your own writing career on the side of what you already do for a job is that you get to create your author life exactly as you wish to live it.

Trust that the breadcrumbs will lead you there

You don't need to know everything that needs to be known right now. If you follow your desire and start writing, the next step will appear when it is needed. And the next, and the next.

Keep that vision in mind of your successful author life and what it looks like. Dream about it often. Be excited that it is coming true right before your eyes. Write what fills your heart with joy; let the words flow; show the world what you want to say. It's fine, you have permission! Go do it!

Chapter 17
Why I chose Amazon to publish my books

The next question after the traditional or self-publishing one, is where is the best place to publish your book? I have chosen to publish on Amazon, however, there are other options including Apple's iBooks, Smashwords, Google Play as well as hosting on your own blog or website.

I have other platforms such as iBooks and Smashwords on my ideas list to try but, well, I've just never gotten around to it. When I already have so many things I want to do with my time – including writing new books, it's just one more thing on my to-do list. I want to keep my life simple, so I focus on just one market place for now, but I also know that I have other options if I ever do want to branch out. I love having possibilities available to me and knowing that I will never have an empty *Ideas* list.

In saying that, I have come across authors online giving opinions such as iBooks being quite difficult to work with and Smashwords no longer being as popular with book purchasers as it used to be. So perhaps my ~~laziness~~ wait-and-see-approach has paid off.

I am a big believer in Pareto's 80/20 rule, which applies to so many different facets of life, and I think it applies to book publishing also. That is, 80% of my income could come from 20% of my effort, which is focusing on the largest sales platform. I could expend much more effort by going with other platforms as well, but not reap much more in the way of rewards simply because they have far less foot traffic. This is purely unscientific because I have not worked out the actual numbers, but anecdotally it works out for me. I have proven it with my Payhip platform (detailed further on in this chapter).

Funnily enough, even though I 'only' publish on Amazon, I have seen my paperback books for sale on other websites such as Barnes & Noble, Book Depository and likely others I don't know about.

I also know my books are in many public libraries around the world, plus readers have told me they have seen my books in retail stores here and there. Libraries and businesses are permitted to bulk-purchase print copies from Amazon at a special wholesale rate.

Because I only uploaded them to Amazon, nowhere else, I feel safe that any royalties owed to me will make their way into my bank account, because I'm sure Amazon keeps a track on money. You don't get to be one of the biggest companies in the world by being sloppy with payments. (And I have always been paid the correct amounts.)

So you don't have to worry that your books will *only* be available on Amazon even if you choose Amazon exclusively. I didn't do a thing to get my books into Barnes & Noble, Book Depository or anywhere else yet they are still there, earning me royalties and finding me new readers as well.

A quick Google search showed that Amazon has fully two-thirds of the online book market, in both print and eBook. Two-thirds! And it's not just because they are an aggressive monopoly (as some say), it's that they provide a great service too.

When I want to browse books and find something new, Amazon is the first place I go to because they have reader reviews, links to the author's blog, a sample of the book to read instantly, and my favourite 'readers who liked this also bought' feature, which has helped me find new authors I love.

When I go to other book retail websites there are none of these things, so I am buying somewhat blind, and I would only order a book if I knew I really wanted it. Amazon has a very user-friendly purchasing process for readers too, and I'd guess that all these reasons are why they are the first choice for most avid readers.

Because of these reasons, and my own good experience, I would happily recommend anyone to start their self-publishing career with Amazon.

I do have one caveat though. I am well aware that putting all my eggs in Amazon's basket means I am at their mercy. If at some stage in the future they drastically change how they pay authors, or really limit how I publish my books, I would have to consider other avenues. I know this, and I still choose to carry on as I am.

I may have be sorry about it tomorrow, or I may live out the rest of my life happily publishing on Amazon and creating my own work-from-home self-employment. I have learned for myself that it doesn't pay to worry about things that may never happen, so I still write confidently and regularly towards the asset base that is my collection of books.

My Payhip experience

Payhip is a great website where you can have your own eStore at no upfront cost. Their only fee is 5% per sale, and for this they provide you with your own storefront, host all your files and take care of European VAT, so you don't get into trouble with the global tax man.

It's a good place to try something different, but really, I have sold a few dozen books *ever* on Payhip, whereas I have sold almost forty thousand books on Amazon.

The only reason for me to still have a Payhip store is because there are a handful of readers who cannot order my eBooks through Amazon in their country (Malaysia being one of them, as I found out when a reader emailed me), plus I have a few other information products listed on Payhip which I am not able to sell on Amazon – audio products such as my *Slimming Success Thoughts* affirmations and *Thirty Chic Days* audiobook, plus my home study eCourse *Create Your Dream Life as a Successful Author*.

If you live in the United States or United Kingdom, you can upload your own recorded audiobooks to Audible, but it doesn't extend to other countries such as New Zealand, where I live. Boo!

I would love to do more of my books in audio format, so I hope this changes soon. I record them with my iPhone voice recorder, and it produces a great sound. If you do live in countries where you can sell your audiobooks through Audible, it would be an excellent addition to your offerings once you have published your book.

Getting started with KDP

Amazon's self-publishing arm is a company called KDP which stands for Kindle Direct Publishing. (You can find it at kdp.com). Before you complete (or even start) your book I'd recommend you sign up for an account with KDP.

It's free to join, and I know from experience that by the time you finish the writing and editing of your book, and put together the cover and marketing blurbs, filling out online forms and setting up your KDP account will feel like the straw that broke the camel's back.

Imagine you've just finished a marathon (let's be positive and make it a half-marathon, I don't want to put you off writing your book) and as you cross the finish line the official says, 'Right, you need to carry on running until you get to the next town, it's only a couple of extra miles'. 'Nooooo!', I hear you cry out, 'I thought I was finished!'

So do yourself a favour and start an account sooner rather than later. It won't take long and because you're going in fresh it will be a breeze. Then, when you're all ready to publish your beautiful and perfectly-formed manuscript, you will be familiar with the KDP website and have one less barrier to achieving your goal of publishing your book.

The other benefit of doing this is that *you will feel like you're already a real author* when you have a KDP account – even if you've only written a few chapters and can't imagine ever completing a whole book. This is because you are going through the motions – the famous 'acting as if' – of publishing a book. You are familiarizing yourself with the process and it will be easier next time.

It gives your scared mind faith that what you are doing is real and it's okay. If you find yourself backing off and saying that it feels too big (it did for me when I was filling in all the financial and tax information), soothe yourself by saying, 'It's okay, you don't have to go through with publishing a book, just fill in these forms. We might never need them!'

Then, when you're finished, you'll feel amazing and wonder what all the fuss was about.

Go to KDP.com now and sign in as a new user, then follow the prompts to complete any necessary information. If you already have an Amazon account you might not even need to create a new login. Amazon is huge because it makes things easy for not only the reader, but the author as well.

Be brave, I know you can do it!

Successful author action tips:

Start your account

Don't wait another day! As soon as you can, log in and create a profile. Even if you don't have time to complete everything, make a start. I promise you it will make a difference to your motivation. You may even find you procrastinate starting your book less.

The way I see it is that you want to **remove as many barriers to writing and publishing as you can**. Break them down a little at a time and before you know it you will (literally) be in business.

Act as if you are a published author to become that published author.

Chapter 18
Pricing your book for success

Amazon offers two different royalty rates for Kindle books – 35% and 70%. (These figures are correct at the time of writing, and have been the same for the five years I have been self-publishing, but please do check for yourself that this is still the case when you are uploading your Kindle book for publication.)

When you price your book between $2.99 and $9.99, you receive 70% in royalties (these are all in US dollars, by the way). If you are lower or higher than this band, you only receive 35%.

So, if you want to try out a tester book and offer it at 99 cents, you will receive around 35 cents royalty per book purchased. But if you price your book at $2.99 you will receive $2.10 per book.

It's a toss-up between pricing your book low enough

that readers will take a chance on you as a new author, and being compensated fairly for your work. There is no set way to price books, and it's quite a fascinating thing to consider whether you go for a lower price and more sales, or a higher price and higher royalty, but less sales.

With my first tester books I priced them at 99 cents for a Kindle copy, and sold what I considered a lot (624 copies in my first month). 99 cents is an easy purchase to make for readers. However, I wasn't making much per book.

After a few months I raised my price to $1.49 to see what would happen. Sales slowed a little. But I was still only earning 35% royalty. The next month I thought 'I wonder what would happen if I raised my prices to $2.99' so I could take advantage of the much higher – doubled – royalty amount. Sales dropped dramatically which made me think twice about my move, but my royalties doubled.

From this pricing change I had half the number of readers but twice as much income. 35% of $1.49 is a royalty of 52 cents per book. 70% of $2.99 is a royalty of $2.09. See the difference?

It might sound callous to do this, but what I realized afterwards is that I hadn't shut out readers who wanted to read my book and now could not afford to; I had simply lost the readers who were only buying cheap books and may not even read them.

Most people likely can afford a $2.99 book, but when something is 99 cents, it's almost a no-brainer. But do you actually value and read a book like that? My Kindle is littered with 99c books that I've never even opened, but if I want a book enough to pay $2.99 or more, I will read it!

Again, going back to my ever-present message of 'it's your books, do what you like with them', perhaps you like the thought of 99 cent books that are downloaded often. Because there is definitely more chance of them being read if they are on someone's Kindle, than if they are not.

The Kindle Unlimited program

One thing I would say from my own experience is not to bother with signing up for KDP Select (for your books to be part of Kindle Unlimited). When I first started self-publishing with Amazon in 2015, I enrolled my books in this Amazon program, and it was great. I was paid a small royalty each time a Kindle Unlimited subscriber downloaded one of my titles at no cost to them. The way Amazon worked their royalties out at the time, was that I was being paid almost as much for my free books as for my normally priced books.

A few months later Amazon changed the way they paid authors for the free books: by pages read versus the book being downloaded. My KDP Select payments dropped to almost nothing, so my income halved overnight. This showed me that people may not necessarily value free books and possibly never get around to reading them. So as soon as the minimum enrolment time had passed, I unenrolled my books from KDP Select and have never gone back.

But, just like with pricing, there is no right or wrong way. If you want to, why not enrol your book in KDP Select and see what happens? You might find it great for you. And that's the cool thing about being your own boss, you can try things to see what you prefer and what works for you. And also change back if you want to.

How I settled on my book prices

I decided to price my longer books as high as I could while still receiving the 70% royalty, which is $9.99. I think they're worth that, and they also benchmark favourably with other similar books. I then priced my smaller books slightly lower, roughly depending on their page count.

You don't have to do this, but that's what felt right for me. As I have mentioned before, I don't like to offer big discounts or drop the price after people have bought my book because I don't like it when that happens to me.

When I have bought something, say a Kindle book or an eCourse, it really upsets me to see a big sale announcement 'get my Kindle book free today!' –

'eCourse 80% off this weekend only!' so I won't do that to other people.

The only way my prices go is UP, if they change, so I make sure I am happy with the price before I set it.

When I first put my original content books out, they were $1 cheaper than they are now, so that's a strategy you could consider – putting your new book out slightly lower in price than you want, then raise it.

You encourage readers to buy your great-priced book and thank them for being early readers, then once you have some reviews under your belt you can raise the price.

In saying all that, I tried my first ever Black Friday sale while writing this book, just to see what would happen. I have been trusting my intuition more and I got the thought that I could have a one-off Black Friday offer with all of my Kindle books priced at $2.99 each.

The idea gave me a buzz of excitement, so I went ahead with it. Sales went through the roof, and even though I was making only a small amount per book, my income was higher because of the number of books sold.

Amazingly (to me), not one person complained that they had bought my books at full price and now there was a special offer. I really thought I would get complaints! I suppose sales are such a part of our life that I really need to get over myself.

After the Black Friday sale was over, I decided to

price my most expensive books at $7.99 rather than $9.99. When I buy a Kindle book, a $9.99 price point requires consideration, whereas I have slightly less resistance to a $6.99 or $7.99 book. I waited until I had a month of sales data, then compared it to before the sale when the prices were higher. I decided that if I sold a lot more books, I'd keep them at the lower price point. If sales were much the same however, I might as well go back to the old, higher price because my readers were going to buy the book anyway.

What I found out was that my income increased by 3% which isn't a lot, but at least it didn't decrease. However, my book numbers were up by 17%. With this information I was happy to keep my books at their new slightly lower price point, because it means I'm not losing out on any earnings and my books are being seen by more people. That can only mean good things.

A few months later, I did the same exercise and found that book numbers had settled to exactly the same as with the higher price, and my earnings were lower. This exercise showed me that a $1 or $2 difference in price didn't necessarily make a difference to my reader, so I increased my book prices to their original value, and they are there to stay.

It's quite invigorating when you see that you are in total control of your own destiny, your own business and you make the final decisions for everything. You are running your own little company, creating the products you sell and increasing your income over time. And it all starts with deciding that you want to write a book.

Getting paid

KDP pays out sixty days after your book is sold (providing you reach the minimum thresholds). For example, for book sales in January, you will receive payments at the end of March.

You will receive several payments from Amazon – one each from all the countries you have sold your books in for the month – Amazon.com, Amazon.co.uk, Amazon.com.au etc – there are thirteen in total and the currencies vary.

The thresholds are quite high - USD$100, 100 GBP, 100 Euros etc. This means that in the beginning you may not be paid straight away for your work, but don't worry, you will eventually.

Some of my markets, such as the US and UK, I am paid out every month, and some less frequently – every two or three months. I was even paid out for one market – Brazil – for the first time in the whole time I have been writing – four years! All the little amounts added up and finally I received a payment. It was quite exciting.

Please don't let me put you off though, I know you want to be paid for your work but in some cases a little patience is required. It's like starting a snowball rolling; as it gains momentum it will pick up more coating. In the beginning, just as with any business, you need to put the effort in to start that momentum and then keep it going.

If you go the traditional publishing route, yes, you will receive a small advance straight away if they choose to sign your book up, however it could then be years before you receive anything else. So believe it or not, self-publishing is actually quicker, even if you do have to wait to reach some thresholds.

Successful author action tips:

Be excited about your earning potential and be realistic at the same time. Don't let your hopes drop when haven't earned $1,000 in the first week.

Be patient and just keep writing. The more books you release, the more you will earn. Play the long game. The more you blog and post on social media, the more people can find out about you, the more books you will sell.

Track your sales and figures regularly (dollars and book numbers). For a long time I tracked daily, but then started tracking less often. I am back to daily tracking again and it's great. It is motivating to see sales, and I love to look back on previous months and see that the numbers are growing. I now have five years of data and every so often I'll look back at it.

It still amazes me that this has happened – I've created a full-time income for myself, doing my most favourite thing ever. And it is possible for you too!

Chapter 19
How to market your book for free

When you are starting out you don't have tons of money to spend because, after all, you are self-publishing not only because you have a dream of being an author, but also because you want to earn money.

Most people assume that it will be out of their financial reach to write and publish a book, and I get it; self-publishing can be expensive when you go through the traditional route of having hundreds or even thousands of copies printed, and that's after paying someone to format and prepare it.

One lady I know personally, spent $47,000 self-publishing her book and she said it had probably cost her to publish rather than actually make any money from the book. Another example I heard about, an author I know of, said she spent $100,000 working with a book coach to write a book that would get onto the NY Times bestseller list. Before that happened though, she abandoned the plan because all the hoops she'd have to jump through didn't feel right to her. $100,000! Spent with no result!

I know it feels amazing to publish a book, undoubtedly, but I wouldn't pay for the privilege. In my opinion, a book has to earn its keep. If it's costing you, it may be more of a vanity or personal project rather than a viable business/create-your-own-job opportunity or career option.

As a new author I didn't have spare money to hire all sorts of people to do everything for me such as book cover design, editing, formatting, marketing etc. And actually it's hugely satisfying to do things yourself; I still enjoy doing it. In addition, I am the kind of person who likes to live lightly, and by not spending too much, I don't need to make a lot of money to live.

How I have done things so far is to spend nothing unless I had no other alternative. In the beginning I bootstrapped this new writing career of mine because I didn't have money to throw around; I wanted to make money instead.

What I wanted to do and what I'm sure you are keen to do as well, was to write and self-publish books to replace my full- or part-time job. That was and still is my goal. I would be the happiest girl around if I never had to complete another job application again, and instead continue to write books from my home office (with my pets as colleagues).

Can I let you know how much it cost me to publish and promote my first books?

$0

That's right. All it took was a bit of know-how (and I was pretty green then, but keen to learn) plus a burning desire to create something for myself. I wanted to see my name up in lights (that might be stretching it, I was keen to see my name up on Amazon) and have my books downloaded by people all around the world. And if I did a good job those people would like what they read and come back for my next book, and my next.

I have a few favourite free tools for self-publishing success which I will go through in this chapter. There are so many fabulous free services on the Internet, but if you don't know about them, they may as well not exist. In addition, how do you know which ones to trust?

More dash than cash

There are tons of ways you can spend lots of money on making yourself known. There are billboards, and magazine and television advertisements, but these days, even big companies with even bigger pockets have had to get smart with how they advertise to their customers.

The Internet is changing *everything* at a lightening pace, so even if you did have loads to spend on advertising your book, there is a good chance that you would still do all the things I'm about to outline.

Crazily enough, I think we are in a more fortunate position than well-established authors, because they are having to unlearn all they've ever known, and begin to do things exactly the same way as you and I.

I've read about popular, established authors grumbling that their managers want them to start blogging or posting on a social media account 'because it personalizes them to their readers'.

So funny, when this is what loads of us have been doing for years just for fun! And I know in my case, it was a happy accident that I already had a readership when I started writing my books.

The world really is changing... hugely. You and I have the chance to reach out directly to our readers and engage with them, creating a living for ourselves alongside traditionally published authors. Even though it boggles my mind, it is a thrilling prospect and I now know that it is more than possible.

Know that this is real, and it's big, and it all starts with your enthusiasm, your desire to write, and a little reaching out to your ideal readers.

Blogging

Back when I started blogging in 2010, it was the main place for me to write. Social media was not really on my radar, and I enjoyed creating my own mini-magazine on my *How to be Chic* blog through blogger.com. It was free to join and easy to set up.

I still maintain my blog at howtobechic.com simply because I've had it for a long time and readers follow me there. If I was starting out today however, I'd probably focus on social media. I'd pick a favourite (currently Instagram) and keep things simple by building that up, rather than trying to do everything at once.

Over time you may wish to add extra platforms on, but to start with, pick one and do it well.

If you do decide to start a blog as a place to give readers a taster of your writing style, there are many great tutorials online. Information changes so rapidly, so if I gave a step-by-step account of how to set up a blog, it would probably be out of date by the time you read this book. Search for a phrase such as 'How to set up a blog' and go with the most recent information presented.

Just briefly though, here is how I did mine:

- Saw that the blogs I loved to read were either on Wordpress or Blogger

- Chose Blogger and joined up there
- Chose a template and colours I liked from their selection
- Started writing
- Tweaked as I went along

When you set up your blog, make it exactly as you'd like it to look, and to suit your personal style. Every little part of what you do, from the way you write, to how your blog and book covers look, all tell your story. They give your reader a sense of what to expect.

It could be a feeling too. For me, I want my blog and writing to be soothing, calm, peaceful, inspiring, creative and fun, because those are the kinds of feelings I am most bolstered by.

When I set up my blog *How to be Chic*, I envisioned a pretty, feminine place where women could come to feel inspired, renewed and uplifted. I also wanted a place that I would look forward to writing at.

I have purposely kept things simple with my blog over the years because I wanted to focus more on my writing. Some thrive on changing their blog look often, and if that's you I say go for it, but for me I would rather spend more time writing than re-doing my blog.

Using images on your blog

When it comes to posting on your blog, you will want to use pictures. Pictures really elevate a blog post. They add colour, impact and a sense of what the post is conveying before someone has even read a word.

I use my own images mostly, though in the beginning I used a lot of stock photos. One big warning is to be careful about photos. It's a big no-no to use other people's photos without giving them credit and you can get into trouble if you use watermarked photos from stock photo companies such as Getty Images.

With phones having fantastic cameras these days, it's not such a big deal because it is so easy to snap photos as you come across pretty flowers, nature scenes or pleasing vignettes in your surroundings. Doing this means you are building up a bank of your own photos to prettify your blog with.

There are places to find images if you are stuck for a picture though, such as unsplash.com, who offer royalty-free photos that you can do what you want with, no attribution needed. But I would encourage you to use your own photos wherever possible. It gives your online presence a more personal look, rather than being too generic.

Blog versus book: what to write where?

You may wonder what material to put in your book and what to put on your blog. Is it the same or different? If someone can read your blog for free, why would they buy your book?

How it's worked out for me is that my books are a

continuation of my blog (and social media).

There are many readers who will just read my blog and never buy my books, and that's fine by me.

But there are also those who love my work so much that they will want *everything* I produce, which means they will buy my books as well as read my blog. Whenever I release a new title, there is a big spike in books ordered, so this means I have a fan base ready to consume whatever it is I have to offer.

If you consistently write on your blog and social media, and write material for your books as well, you will build this up over time – provided you write about what really lights you up.

But what to put where, though? Here are some ideas to consider:

- Having a short blog post on a topic (say, 300-500 words) versus a lengthier essay on the same topic for your book (1,500-2,000 words.)

- Making your blog about current events and what you are up to, versus your book being about topics you want to explore.

- Having your blog posts be videos or podcasts, and all your writing going into your books.

- Only having social media which are photos and short captions, and putting all of your writing into your books (so, no blog or website at all.)

There is no one way to approach this. You can see what feels good to you. Looking at the examples above, I mostly do the first point: shorter posts on favourite topics, then expand on those topics for my book writing.

I also mix in a little of the second point: talk about what's current in my life. It's up to you how personal you get, but whichever way you go, your readers want to get to know *you*.

Social media

Chances are, you already belong to some or all of the main social media platforms such as Facebook, Instagram and Twitter. Even if you might not think you're 'a Facebook person', for example (I didn't, back in the day), all these platforms are so useful for marketing.

Consider this: you can advertise yourself for free on them. *Free advertising*!

If you don't have a social media presence around what you want to write on, you are hiding your light under a bushel, and no-one can find out about you, or your book once you've written it.

Don't wait until you have published your book to

start letting people know you exist either; start today. Build your following as you write, let people get to know you and what you love to write about, bring them along on your journey as you write your book. By giving them little testers of your writing, they will fall in love with you. Then when you hit 'Publish', you will have an audience eagerly waiting to purchase your book.

Instagram.com

If I could choose only one platform to use when it came to social media, it would be Instagram. Even though I've had my Facebook profile a lot longer, my Instagram profile quickly overtook it in terms of follower numbers.

It's quicker and easier to use, it's more attractive and cleaner looking visually, and uploading a post is as easy as taking a photo and adding a few words. And hashtags, you will always want to remember the hashtags.

Download the Instagram app from the App Store on your phone and join today. Even if you don't post on it straight away it will be there for you when you are ready. You can start following accounts you like and you will find that people will start following you too.

When you do come to post, think about how you want your Instagram page to look. I like mind to be personal and friendly, with a mix of pets, home style, outfits, meal ideas and pretty things. My goal is to inspire, and also talk about my books. When I post a photo, I check my Instagram page to ensure a pleasing mix of image types. I wouldn't post ten meal ideas in a row, or outfit after outfit etc. It might be a cute dog photo one day, an outfit the next, and a book I'm enjoying after that. It just takes a quick glance at your page to ensure you are happy with it.

You can use up to thirty hashtags per post, so use all of them as often as you can. Doing this will help readers find you. I have an 'Instagram Hashtag' file on my computer where I keep all the hashtags I use, plus note down ideas for new ones as I hear about them or dream them up.

You can do research about how to choose good hashtags, but for me personally I don't want to spend hours doing that when I could be writing. I'll do a few quick Internet searches, then get back to my writing.

When people comment, 'heart' their comment and reply as much as you can. It's especially important when you are growing your audience, plus you have more time to do it then. Now that I am getting more and more to do with my writing, I want to spend less time on Instagram. Still, I heart all my comments and reply to the ones that need replying to.

Keeping in touch with people is vital, plus it's quite fun with Instagram.

Facebook.com

To be able to have a 'business' page for your books on Facebook, you need to have a personal profile uploaded. My personal profile is there purely because I wanted an author page. I don't use Facebook in my private life at all. I share everything on my author page that I do on my blog and Instagram. I also interact with readers on Facebook.

When you post on Instagram, you can opt to have your photo and caption automatically posted on Facebook too. I use this feature all the time, because, why not? It saves me doing the same job twice, and even though there will be some people on both Instagram and Facebook, many will only be on one or the other so it makes sense to post the same information to both.

Twitter.com

I am on Twitter because I thought I should have a profile there. Some days I wonder why I am there if it's not my thing, but then I think, 'Well what if some of my readers are *only* on Twitter and no-where else, how will they find out about me then?' and that keeps me tweeting.

Like Facebook, there is an Auto option available when you are posting on Instagram.

Or, if you want more than a link on Twitter, it only

takes a few minutes to upload a photo I have already used on a blog post or social media, with a link to my blog post, or a shortened version of my social media caption.

But the auto-link option in Instagram is better than nothing if I don't have the time or energy to do a separate tweet.

Mailchimp.com

Even though you might have followers on social media, these people aren't really 'yours'. They belong to the company who provides the platform, such as Facebook or Instagram and as such, can be taken away from you in an instant.

The only contacts you truly 'own' are the emails on your newsletter list, which is why it's important to start building this list up. Yes, people can unsubscribe, and there are strict anti-spam laws (rightly so), but if you respect your readers and their Inbox, most people will be happy to stay on your email list.

Then, when you have your new book ready for release you can let everyone on your list know about it, with a link to purchase, of course.

I use an email newsletter system from Mailchimp to connect with my readers. It's simple to use and has easy templates you can customize. For example, with my *How to be Chic* newsletters, I have made the background the same pink as my blog. This provides a pleasingly cohesive 'brand recognition', and it looks pretty too.

Mailchimp is free until you reach 2,000 subscribers. It took me quite a while to get to 2,000 and I was nervous about paying a monthly subscription after that, but by the time I did get to 2,0000 I was earning money so I didn't mind at all (and it's a very reasonable monthly fee in my opinion, starting at $30). In fact I was amping myself on to get to 2,000 because it felt like a success milestone to have to pay because I had so many people on my mailing list. I thought this was a nice way to reframe, 'Oh no, I have to pay now!'

But in the beginning, I made full use of my free Mailchimp account and it helped me grow my audience by sharing blog posts and book releases with my readers.

To encourage readers to join your list, it is helpful to have a link on your blog or social media page offering a freebie. For mine, I have free excerpts of all my books in PDF format, and an exclusive '21 ways to be chic' audio recording and transcript that can't be obtained from anywhere else i.e. it's not on my blog and you can't buy it.

It is a one-time-thing to set this up on Mailchimp.

I also have automated Mailchimp to send a newsletter out whenever a new post goes up on my blog – the whole post is sent to my subscribers in an email. I used to only put the first couple of paragraphs in the email, then direct readers back to my blog, but I changed it to include the whole newsletter. Personally I would rather read a whole article in an email instead of having to click and link, so I thought others might too. The main thing is that you want your reader to view the whole blog post, so why not make it easy for them?

Canva.com

Canva is a fantastic website where you can make your own social media posts, banners and covers, blog images and headers; even Kindle book covers. There are loads of free templates that look polished and professional, and you can upload your own images to personalize them as well. I use the free version of Canva to make my own images, both with free stock photos and photos taken by me.

There's also a great 'colour find' tool on Canva. Simply upload a photo or image that you love the colours of, and you will find out the main shades and their official six-digit codes. Doing this will give you a colour palette to base your brand around or decorate your blog with. It's really fun! You can find it here:

https://www.canva.com/color-palette/

Or search for 'canva color palette'. The Canva Color Palette Generator should be the first thing that pops up.

Canva is intuitive to use; I've had no graphic design experience and it's fun to have a play around and make your own images. Their templates look very designery, and you can change the fonts, colours and backgrounds to suit your style.

Successful author action tips:

Choose your focus and start an account today. Do it on a whim; many of my best decisions have been made this way.

When I started my blog *How to be Chic*, it was spontaneous, and almost tongue-in-cheek, because I was not a fashion plate. Instead, my own personal style is simple, classic, down-to-earth, pretty and practical. But then that blog became my brand as I explained my way of thinking to my readers.

While you're there, why not post something? Introduce yourself, say why you love your chosen topic(s) and keep things light-hearted and fun. There is no seriousness required.

Use your writing to inspire your blog and social media, and the other way around too. If you're stuck on one, write on the other. You'll soon become unclogged!

Chapter 20
How to gain readership for your blog and social media pages

Getting more eyes on your blog or social media page is all down to posting consistently, but it's also about interacting with others. Whether it's a blog, Instagram or Facebook page, here are my top tips to increase your following:

- Comment on others blogs that have a similar audience to you. Be authentic and genuine. I never find it hard to be authentic because the kinds of blogs that are similar to mine, I also love to read as well!

- On a blog, have a 'blogroll' listing blogs you love – others may reciprocate by putting you on theirs. I've never asked anyone to include mine, but you may be bolder than me.

- Start a Facebook and Instagram page for your blog, or one that is geared towards your blog. If your blog/book topics are truly something you are interested in, they will naturally be part of your life anyway. Show behind the scenes, daily images, etc.

- If people start following you, take a look at their blog or social media page and start following them if they look like your market. I don't follow people when they are very obviously just spamming themselves around (i.e. a get-rich-quick or weight-loss-in-a-week account).

- Be consistent. Blog a minimum once each week. Some do more, but I find for me that once a week is a good frequency. You can blog as little or as much as you like, but less than once a week I lose my momentum and may lose readers, and more than once a week I find takes away from my other writing.

- Pin your blog or social media images to your Pinterest page. People will come across them there who may not follow you on any other platform.

- Consider a blog or social media series. When I came up with *30 Chic Days*, the blog series, it was an impulsive decision to post about all the little things that made me feel chic.

  I didn't know how I was going to do a blog post every day for thirty days (and it nearly killed me each time I did that series!), but I committed and then followed through.

  Not only was it good training for my stickability, but my online traffic and readership went *through the roof*, both that month and afterwards. In addition, it sparked the idea for my first original book; I had no idea that would happen, but I am so grateful it did.

  If a month is too long, try 7, 10, 14 or 21 days as a challenge or series. (I did a seven-day 'Week of Beauty' series on my blog as well.)

Go with what feels good. For me it feels good to build my followers slowly and sustainably with people who are 'my kind of people' – lovely ladies who enjoy living a nice life.

Sometimes things I've done in the past haven't felt right; for example, an online friend told me of a women's writers group on Facebook that had thousands of members. They had a 'follow each other' day of the week. I participated for a few weeks to give it a try. The reasoning is that it looks better if you have more followers than less.

I followed tons of female authors and many followed me, but it was a bit hit or miss and I didn't really have any new possible readers because we were all writing completely different types of books therefore liked to *read* different types of books. It felt like a fake way to have more followers although I did find a couple of new fiction authors that I loved so it wasn't a total bust!

If I was going to focus on growing my followers now I would do it by posting more frequently, following back the people who followed me ('my people' only, not fitness and Internet marketing spammers), and following people who like accounts similar to mine.

How to build and keep momentum

If there was a magic word to marketing, it's CONSISTENCY as I've said before. It might sound boring and unnecessary, after all, you want to post when you are struck by the muse, and having to post regularly could become tiresome.

Let's turn the camera around though, so you are on the other side, looking in.

Imagine you have a favourite shop in town. It sells items that make you happy. When you go there they have the most beautiful music playing. The lady who owns the store is adorable and she is always happy to see you and greets you like an old friend, even if you haven't been in for a while. She gives great service and her prices are reasonable. There's no other way to say it – you have a shop crush!

However.

She is inconsistent with her opening hours. You go there on a Saturday afternoon for a browse when she has been open before, but the store is closed. The next week when you call by she says, 'Oh, it was such a nice day I decided to get out into the garden instead.'

Because you have been disappointed so often by her being closed when she was meant to be open, you gradually stop visiting and end up forgetting about her.

That's exactly what happens to inconsistent online presences. We all know those blogs that start off with great promise. A beautiful website and a focus or topic that you love. But, you might see five posts in one week, two posts the next, nothing for two months then an apologetic post explaining that the blogger has been caught up in life.

This my friends, is a hobby blogger. And you are not a hobby blogger. Your blog (or social media account, whichever you choose) is part of your new career. And when you start treating every part of your writing as your new business venture, it will flourish.

The combination of inspirational writing + consistent effort is unbeatable!

The key is not to promise too much. I see bloggers announcing that they will be posting Monday, Wednesday and Friday and I think to myself 'Gee, once a week posting comes around quickly enough for me.' And then they burn out.

Start off with once a week for a blog post, or three times a week for social media. Ideally social media would be once a day, but it can be a lot to come up with. I used to stress myself about it, worrying that I wasn't posting enough, but where does it stop?

Big successful Instagram accounts post a minimum of three times a day, sometimes more, but I reminded myself that social media is only part of my marketing plan, not my whole business plan. Some only have Instagram as their thing so it makes sense that they'd do more, and the same with blogs.

Really successful blogs put out substantial blog posts every day of the week. But for me, I again reminded myself that all of these things are only the bit part characters in my author career and that *the writing comes first*. I'm not getting paid for social media; I *am* getting paid for writing my books.

Don't worry if you don't think you're doing enough. By all means do something, but be happy with that. If you already post quite regularly on social media and enjoy it, carry on, but don't make yourself miserable worrying that you should be doing more. I've tried that myself and it doesn't work! Instead, when I gave myself a break and decided that a minimum level was enough, I felt more inspired to post.

How to be consistent then? Decide what you're going to do and stick to it, no matter what. If you're going on vacation, plan ahead. If you know you will be busy on the day you do your posting, do it ahead of time.

For me, I create a blog post once a week and I do additional social media updates throughout the week. Once a week may not sound like much to you, or it may sound like a lot. For me it's the perfect balance of being present and visible without spending all my time writing blog posts.

I don't get paid for blog and social media posts, they are like my marketing or advertising (not completely, because they are still fun for me, but you get my drift). I get paid for writing my books and information products, so if I spend all my time doing things I don't get paid for, I would have to go and get a job and then I'd have less time for everything.

I would recommend a minimum of once per week for your main piece of free content, but you can choose. Whatever you do, be consistent about it! You want to be seen as steady, stable, always there, and to be relied upon. You don't want to be seen as flaky, fly-by-night, unreliable, and you definitely don't want people to forget about you.

If you choose not to have a blog, decide how many Facebook and Instagram posts you want to do. Instead of spending one day a week doing your blog posts, you might divide that time up and do once or twice a day social media posts instead.

You can change how you do things too – if you draw

up a schedule to try and it doesn't work easily for you, why not change it up. Start then tweak, keep going, and you will build your readership person by person.

Successful author action tip:

If you do have **an unintended period away** from your blog or social media, don't come back with an apologetic, 'I've been so busy!' and then promise an unrealistic schedule going forward. I have seen this so many times and it stresses me out just reading it, because I have been there too!

Instead, simply come back and carry on as if you had never been away. Trust me, it looks better and you will feel less flaky. Just continue on with the topics you love to talk about, and **everything will work out fine**.

Chapter 21
Just start!

The most important message I have for you is to *just start*. Somewhere. Anywhere. You don't have to have the perfect idea, enough money to build a beautiful website, or learn the perfect way to write. Action trumps perfection every time.

Don't think about it too much, just do it. Take one small step, then another, and another. You can jump in anywhere – with the actual book writing, or posting online which will become your marketing. Let people know you exist.

Right now really is the best time to start – you are not too early or too late. You haven't missed the boat. You are the perfect age too – how wonderful!

I started at 44 and within a few years had created a full-time income for myself.

If you are young, don't think you're 'too young to write a book' either. Imagine if you started your first book at twenty-two? If you disregarded thoughts from yourself or others that you were too young, imagine how far ahead you would be at your current age now.

My thirteen-year-old niece loves horses and reads a series of horse books popular with young girls. She also loves to write. I said to her, 'Do you think you could write a horse book too?' Her eyes lit up, 'Yes!' So, I encouraged her to start her first horse book and she did – on a Google doc that she shared with me. It was such a cute story.

It doesn't matter if you begin something then put it away because you have come to your senses and seen that clearly you will never be any good. Ha, did you see what I did there? I tricked you! That was a clear lie, because really, what is 'good'? As I have already mentioned in *Chapter 10*, there are plenty of terrible books that are number-one bestsellers.

Not that I'm saying your book is terrible but imagine if you didn't listen to your inner critic, finished the book and published it. Who knows what amazing things might happen off the back of that?

So, if you have a half-written book, get it out of your drawer (or computer file). You may find, as I did with *Thirty Chic Days* that you want to carry on with it, or you might decide to start afresh instead. Both are valid choices – there are no wrong decisions. The only wrong decision is to give up on your dream of becoming an author if you have always desired to be one.

How exciting is it to think that you could be in full control of your job? Not to have to ask the boss for time off or a sick day if you are feeling unwell? I'll tell you, it's wonderful. I am grateful every day that I get to be at home writing my books and doing what I love. I am grateful that I get to visit my mum during the day or take the dogs for a walk between chapters.

And it's a career you can have for a long time too. There is no mandatory retirement age – you can write for as long as you want to. In 2018 novelist Penny Vincenzi died aged 78, part-way through her eighteenth book. Louise Hay had a long writing career and was still writing in her eighties (she died aged ninety in 2017).

I'm sure it keeps your mind young too, all that writing, thinking and reading. I'd surely rather do that than crosswords (no offence to crossword fans!)

All it comes down to is a decision to do it. So start writing. The sooner the better.

Don't wait for the perfect time

It's important to know that you will probably never be ready. You need to start *before* you feel ready. I can hear you saying, 'but I need to do this first, then I'll start'. 'This' might be taking a creative writing class, losing weight or getting healthier, waiting until your children leave home, planning for when life is less busy…

What I have found with anything that is important to me is that it needs to be fitted into my life as it is right now. Would you agree? Otherwise you'll find another year has gone by and you don't know where the time went. All you need to do is take one small step each day or each week. Start that 250 words per day as explained in *Chapter 4*.

Or, set up an Instagram account where you start posting on your favourite topics. You will get a feel for what you would like to write about at the same time as finding your readers. You don't even need to go out and gather them; you will call them in just by being you. All you have to do is show up online and they will find you.

Putting in the extra effort to reach your goal is worth it. This has been a desire of yours for a while. If you want it, it's up to you to make it happen. It's time to get on with it and make your dreams a reality.

You can call yourself a writer today

Identify with being a writer, even if you haven't published anything yet. Everyone has to start somewhere and so do you. When someone asks you what you do, say, 'I'm a writer'. If people ask you what you write, you can honestly say 'I'm working on my first book' or 'I am creatively writing at the moment so I can find out what I best love writing about'.

Plant that 'I'm a writer' seed into your mind and let it take root. Don't make yourself feel like a fraud by saying you are a writer and then not writing. Begin writing straight away and start building up your body of work. Write short pieces, book outlines, dream up little scenarios for yourself, journal inspiration and just keep on writing.

I have written some ideal situations for myself such as the Paris piece in the 'Day 2: Start with a vision' chapter of *Thirty Slim Days* and loved doing so. This was an inspiration piece for myself, and it found a place in one of my books. In the future, who knows, these inspiration pieces may lead onto a novel, because I would love to try fiction too.

(If you want to read my Paris vision piece you should be able to see it in the free 'Look Inside' preview available on Amazon if you don't already have my *Thirty Slim Days* book).

The cool thing is you can take your writing wherever you like. You can start with non-fiction and go into fiction. You can write children's or teen books. You can write a purely practical how-to book and then try something more ethereal. All of my books certainly have a similarity about them, which is great for continuity from the reader's point of view, but if I decided I wanted to try something completely different, I would.

The important thing is not to let any perceived barrier stop you from even giving it a go. Who knows what amazing things you can make happen, and maybe sooner than you think?

Successful author action tips:

Decide right here, as you finish reading this chapter that **you are going to start writing**. You are going to put aside any thoughts of not being good enough and just start. Have in your mind that you are now a writer and that you can't wait to see what your first book will look and feel like.

Decide on a first small step and do it, whether it's writing a blurb for your book to say what it's about, or posting on your blog or social media that you are starting your book. Don't have an online presence? Let's get one set up and do a first post on it.

Don't look back, only forwards. Write and stash, post and carry on. Keep your eyes on the prize: the book you are going to publish and the readers who will order it. You are writing it for them, but you are also writing for yourself. It will feel so good! Let's get going!

100 Ways to Create Your Dream Life as a Successful Author

If you have read any of my other books, you will know how much I love a highly motivating bonus chapter at the end. So let's jump in and get fired up to be a successful author and create our dream life for ourselves. I know you can do it, and I hope that by this stage in the book you do too.

1. **Start today.** The only day you have is today – today is your future! You are a successful woman, and successful women who are going places don't wait until tomorrow. Take one small step towards your dreams *today*.

2. **You can do it.** You will know by now that being an author is entirely possible for you. Keep that thought in mind and affirm often to yourself that it

is achievable. Don't listen to others who have negative thoughts.

3. **Build a strong foundation.** I invite you to think of your writing career as planting a tree for your future. You have to grow big, stable roots to support the tree that is seen above ground. Keep the tree analogy in mind when you are toiling away and know that you are building a strong root system word by word, and hour by hour.

4. **Raise your vibration.** Inspire yourself every day by doing what feels good – journaling, reading a favourite book, making notes from an idea that comes to you, imagining your wonderful future and how amazing it's going to be, appreciating how far you have come already, browsing a gorgeous magazine or glossy picture book, and people-watching. Do it all!

5. **Be out in nature every day** – by going for a walk, having your coffee outside in the morning; even just standing with your face turned to the sun for a few moments if you can't manage anything else. If it's rainy, enjoy the sound of the raindrops and all that goodness soaking into the earth.

6. **Find out the time of day you love to write** and block that time out in your calendar. This is your work time so show people you mean it by writing

at the times you said you were going to. Trial different times of the day and evening if you aren't sure what feels best for you.

7. **Always come back to what you would love to read.** Ask yourself: 'What book/blog/social media post would I love to read right now? Then write that.

8. **Practice your successful author lifestyle as often as you can.** The things that you imagine you'll do 'One day when', do them now. The clothes you see yourself wearing, the words you will say to yourself and others, and the schedule you will keep. Practice all those things now as much as possible.

9. **Keep your budding ideas to yourself**, in your own secret garden. Have them be fully formed before you even breathe a word of them to anyone else. Your ideas need you to do that for them.

10. **Keep yourself nourished**, just as if you were an athlete. You cannot think well if you have not given yourself good protein, fresh fruits and vegetables, and kept yourself hydrated.

11. **Keep your workspace as well-organized as you can** without spending a lot of time doing so. When I have a five-minute tidying blitz on my desk it makes a huge difference to my ability to focus.

12. **Track your sales daily** once you have books listed on Amazon or other eCommerce platforms. When you've made a sale, it is very motivating; if you log in to see that you have sold nothing the previous day, it's a good reminder to get on with it.

13. **Set up work hours**, no matter your current employment situation. Say you are a night owl in a full-time job. Maybe you'll decide to write from 7pm to 9pm, Mondays to Thursdays. It will get you – and your loved ones – into a routine. You can change your hours at any time, too.

14. **If you are procrastinating, find out why.** Often for me it's because I am not enthused enough about what I'm writing. So, I'll either give myself permission to put it aside and start a different project, or, if I know it's something I really want to complete, I will pump myself up beforehand by reading an inspiration piece I have written or journaling something new. It doesn't take long and I'm inspired and ready to go.

15. **Dream big dreams** – even if you don't achieve them all, you will reach further than you might have otherwise. I'll sometimes think things to myself such as, 'If I had 100 books for sale on Amazon – how amazing would that be?' It's exciting to think about!

16. **Keep hydrated** with a big bottle of water on your desk. I found that a glass emptied too quickly, and I didn't want to put a bigger open container on my desk in case one of my cats knocked it over, so I bought myself a one-litre (one quart) water bottle with a lid and a straw for my desk. I am amazed at how quickly I go through it.

17. **Love your back.** If you find your back, neck or shoulders getting stiff from lots of typing, don't ignore it. Pull your shoulders back and down to open up your chest. If you have particularly knotty tight spots like I do, massage that area with a tennis ball against the wall or while lying on the floor.

18. **Curate your successful author wardrobe** by looking at what *she* would wear to write in every day. I have this vision of myself wearing chic, stylish clothes that are comfortable and cozy (in the winter) or cool and airy (in the summer).

19. **Create writing rituals for yourself.** Two of my favourites are: Rising at 6am for hot tea and writing, and after dinner journaling while my husband watches television.

20. **Have a goals notebook** and write down your top ten goals every day – they can be all in one area or a mix of life goals, health goals, relationship goals, money goals and writing goals. When I've done this

consistently it's been so good for my mindset.

21. **Find success mentors who inspire you**, and top up on their inspiration often. They might be in real life, online or in books. I like to list all the ways someone inspires me and the kinds of things they do or how they are. I can then tap into their energy and influence at any time.

22. **Change your focus.** Instead of focusing on how you can write a book that people will like and that will sell well, focus on creating work that you love. You will find your entire energy shift with this one simple change.

23. **Set the timer on your phone** for a period of time that you decide to write for – maybe it's thirty or sixty minutes. Ignore all thoughts of things you have suddenly realized you simply *must* look up on the computer and keep typing. Then, feel proud when the buzzer goes off.

24. **Keep your beautiful future in mind every day.** Know that you will achieve your dream of the perfect lifestyle for you. Imagine how wonderful it's going to be then, and this will make you happy to make the extra sacrifices right now. Have the courage to be different to others.

25. **Identify with being a *creator* rather than a *consumer*.** When I consciously shift my energy

over to that of being more of a creator, it feels so much better. I don't shop or snack as often, and I produce more content.

26. **Ignore the critic in your head.** She hasn't experienced what you dream of before and is only trying to keep you safe and away from the unknown. Doing something new requires a certain amount of determination and blind faith. It is so worth it though.

27. **You are safe today and always.** Even though some steps on this journey feel like stepping out onto a ledge you are not sure exists, you will be fine – more than fine: it will be the making of you. Many others have done it before you; follow them for confirmation that the path you are taking is safe.

28. **Follow my journey and others who resonate with you**, even if their approach is different to yours. I am inspired by ladies who are coaches and it doesn't matter that I am not a coach. Inspiration is inspiration.

29. **Hang around with those who uplift you**, and *be* an uplifting person yourself. Don't bring up depressing stories from the news or something that made you grumpy today. Focus on what's good and think before you speak.

30. **Enjoy yourself when you write.** I always am so much more enthused by my own writing (and it's easier to do) when I'm being a bit loose and free with it. I sit down to write and ask myself, 'What would be so much fun to write about?'

31. **Ask for help from other family members.** Are you cooking dinner every night? Delegate meals and household chores to others and ask that they help you feel supported in your new career choice.

32. **Focus single-mindedly on your greatest goal of the moment**, whether it's writing 2,000 words, brainstorming ten ideas for social media posts or doing the final edit on your first book.

33. **Carry a notebook with you *everywhere*.** Write down your top ten goals each day; chapter ideas for a book; notes and quotes as you come across them; or even a paragraph you've dreamed up.

34. **Start writing on a blank page and see what comes out.** I have a *'Fiona's Journal'* Word document where I do this regularly. Some entries have been illuminating, some have formed great blog posts, and many are highly inspiring to me. I might write a whole page or only a few paragraphs.

35. **Move your body every day.** Go for a walk around your neighbourhood, do a gym workout or take five minutes to stretch on the floor. Even just standing up from your chair, taking deep breaths and stretching your arms above your head is fabulous.

36. **Write in different genres as you feel called to.** I love writing fiction pieces for myself from time to time, and I'd love to do a fiction book one day as I've mentioned. Who knows, by doing this you might just find a whole new genre that you love to write in.

37. **The healthier you are, the higher your vibration** and this inspires you to do more towards success. For me it's making sure I have water on my desk (or a bottle in my car when I have errands to do), getting to bed in good time since I like to rise early, and not eating too much sugar.

38. **Persistence will get you to where you want to go.** Take small actions every day. Be consistent with your work or at least learn to be more consistent. Forgive yourself for an off-day when you don't do anything. Tomorrow is a new day.

39. **Increase your success by increasing your self-worth.** Affirm to yourself, 'I am enough, exactly as I am' and be your own cheerleader while

you are writing. Feel light and buoyant and have fun while you write, and you will be happier with what you create.

40. **Picture your readers as lovely people** who enjoy what you have to say, because I promise you it's the truth. I used to be scared of bad feedback or one-star reviews, but now I don't mind them so much. Everybody is entitled to their opinion.

41. **Look to others who are doing well** with their writing, and see what you can learn from them. If there is an idea I see that I love, I'll add it to my 'Ideas to try' file; if they do something I don't like, I'll mentally file it as something *not* to do.

42. **Decide what makes you feel successful** and do those things more. For me it's things like dressing well, stretching my creativity every day, inspiring myself, and keeping my home tidy and neat most of the time.

43. **Don't downplay your writing.** You don't have to boast about it, but don't put it down either. I try to catch myself whenever I say something unsupportive about my career and skills.

44. **Change your views on discipline** – think of discipline as fun and exciting and that it is the gateway to a fabulous life, whether it is around writing every day, being healthy, or committing to

a social media and blogging schedule.

45. **Fast forward five years in your mind.** You are fabulously successful as an author. Now ask yourself: If I was that successful author *today*, how would I act? Who would I be? Brainstorm everything you can think of that the future you does, and *do that. Today.*

46. **List all the ways you are successful already** – shoot for one hundred! Mix into your list areas in which you aren't successful yet, but wish you were. Blending together your current reality and your ideal future is a fun and powerful way to get you there.

47. **Simplify your life for more abundance** – declutter hot spots, keep your writing desk neat, and get rid of magazines and newspapers once you've read them. You will feel livelier and more motivated when your house is tidy and organized.

48. **Prioritize your most important task of the day** and do it first thing. If it's an hour of writing, do that hour of writing. Imagine if you did this every day; you would still be a roaring success even if you were only 'on top of things' for a short period of time during that day.

49. **Organize food ahead of time** so it's one less thing to think about when you want to focus on

your writing.

50. **Have a day when you don't switch the computer on *at all*.** Usually this will be a weekend day for me, but if I have a weekday where I have errands out and then meet my mum for lunch, I don't turn the computer on when I get home. It refreshes me and I miss my writing, so I can't wait to get stuck in the next day.

51. **Write a brag letter to yourself** of everything you are proud of. Not only will seeing this make you feel good and build up your confidence, but you will also gather useful information for your author bio, and maybe even get ideas for future books or blog posts.

52. **Remove negative words about success from your life** – instead of, 'It will never happen for me – I might as well give up – Who am I kidding?', say 'I am taking small steps everyday towards my goals – As long as I keep on going, I will succeed – Why NOT me?'

53. **When you have a new idea that you love, move quickly.** Put one thing into place or take one action straight away. Whenever I have done this, I have had fantastic results, and I truly believe that little thunderbolts like these are designed to propel us forward – if only we'd take notice of

them.

54. **Surround yourself with people who have a positive mindset** – not only in real life but with the news you watch, books you read, and people you follow on social media.

55. **Create an office space that inspires you.** It doesn't matter if you don't have an office or even a desk of your own yet, start with where you write now, and make it an appealing place to be.

56. **Be your own PR person**, for yourself. When you start receiving happy emails from readers, create a 'Fan Mail' folder in your Inbox. It took a while for me to build this stash up, but even when I had one or two from ladies who read my blog, it was a boost for me.

57. **Make your dream life vision compelling** to you. For days when you are not as motivated, have a mini-film to run in your head. For years, mine was to be a stay-at-home pet mum in our lovely home, writing books from my home office. What is your dream vision? Make up fun and exciting scenarios and pump yourself up with them.

58. **Ask yourself, 'What is the next practical step I can take right now?'** then do that. Just that one next step. When I do this, I am that bit further along, and I feel good.

59. **Inspire yourself in whatever way you can**, because that's how you will get to where you want to go. Suspend reality and *dream*. Ask the Universe, God or whoever you go to and see what happens.

60. **Enrol other people in your vision.** It might be your spouse or partner, another family member, or a supportive friend who also dreams big. Paint a picture of how wonderful it is going to be in the future. Get *them* excited too.

61. **Use envy in a constructive way.** If you find yourself feeling envious of another's achievements, look at how they've gotten there. With my favourite online success mentors, I love to look back at them when they were a lot newer (such as their old YouTube videos or blog posts), which has inspired useful ideas for me.

62. **Write yourself a 'Secrets to my Success' article.** A journalist has asked you to go through everything you've done that has made you the successful author you are today. Write this as the future you and brainstorm all the little details that make up your wonderful lifestyle as an author. I promise you will love the resulting piece.

63. **Let your intuition lead you.** I believe that ideas that pop into your mind seemingly from nowhere

are from inside you, as well as the collective consciousness. More and more I am letting myself be guided by those thoughts and I have had wonderful things happen as a result.

64. **Don't be scared to put out a tester book** before you are ready. Just like I did with my blog post books, is there something short-ish you have written already that you can put up for sale on Kindle for 99c or $2.99? Just to get the practice and 'break the seal' of uploading a book.

65. **Decide to be gutsy.** I would never have written and published a book if I wanted to play safe, because the very thought of it scared the daylights out of me. What's the thing that scares you? Can you at least explore it further, or perhaps take one small side-step towards it?

66. **If social media is scary to you, choose your favourite ONE** and start with that. Forget about all the others and focus on building up your confidence – and readership – with one outlet. Later on you might add one or two more, but don't try to do everything or you'll probably become overwhelmed and do nothing.

67. **What modality do you feel most yourself in?** Is it writing, speaking on video, making audios with your phone... Choose one that you find the

easiest and most fun, and specialize in that. I find it easiest to write, so I mostly write.

68. **Delete habits and thoughts that make you feel deflated** and like a loser. Some thoughts and habits may relate directly to your writing, and others won't. Happily, I find that whenever I clean up one area of my life, it spills over positively into other areas.

69. **Be consistent with whatever you decide your 'thing' is.** Sure you can change it up every so often, but having a certain level of consistency makes your readers feel safe and in good hands, whether they are reading your blog or your books.

70. **Think in terms of books, not book.** What I have found is that when you put out a new book there is a boost in sales, and then they gradually drop each month until they get to a stable level. With each new book you release, you can expect to create a steady base income between books that inches higher each time. This is how you will build a consistent income for your future.

71. **Think about what comes easily to you**, and focus on that. I find it easy to write about living a simple and beautiful life, and all the things I do to achieve that. Why struggle hacking through the overgrown jungle by choosing something hard, if

there is a nice-looking easy trail laid out that you could choose instead?

72. **Identify your key values and live your life by them** – some of mine are freedom, simplicity, peace and creativity. How I bring them into my life is by looking at each one and asking myself 'How can I create more freedom in my life?', 'Where can I simplify things?', 'How can I feel more peaceful?' and 'How can I bring more creativity into my days?' Your values will inspire you writing, as well.

73. **Fall in love with your writing.** This thought came to me when I realized that when I decide that I love something or someone, they or it become more attractive to me. How this applies to your writing is that I want you to really fall in love with it - adore it and infuse it with your love. When you love your writing, others will too.

74. **Don't fall into the trap of stifling your writing time** with marketing time or even worse, busy-work. Yes, blog and post or network on social media, but keep it in its rightful place by only spending a short time on it. Yes, tidy your desk and file your paperwork but keep it to short periods too. Ask yourself when you are doing these sorts of things, 'How fast can I get this done?' and then GO. After that, back to your writing.

75. **If you find that you are struggling** with some aspect of your writing – your schedule, your motivation to write, posting on social media or coming up with blog posts, ask yourself, 'How can I make this easier?' Then, note any answers that come up, or brainstorm a list of ten ways if you can, of how to make whatever it is you're struggling with easier.

76. **Remember your 'why'** – why are you doing what you are doing? Remember the grand vision you have for your life often, and let it lift you and carry you forward.

77. **Forgive yourself for (perceived) mistakes** you've made in the past and trust that where you are now is where you're meant to be.

78. **Look at what you need to upgrade** to move forward as a successful writer. Write everything down that you think is not in the first-class category for you at the moment, then choose one to upgrade right now. It might be something intangible such as your mindset – are you thinking too negatively about your goal? Or it could be something entirely practical, such as when I bought myself a proper office chair to support my back better.

79. **Automate where you can.** Look at everything you do and see how you can automate it: things such as Mailchimp sending a newsletter out based on your blog post, or other social media platforms posting automatically after you post on Instagram (detailed in *Chapter 19*).

80. **Feel excited for your abundant future**, which starts with what you are doing *today*. Keep those good feelings inside you: the feelings of being a published author, reaching others with your words, and earning a living working in *exactly* the way that suits you.

81. **Because YOU are your ideal reader**, you don't have to worry about what others may want to read. As long as you are happy with the topic you have chosen and what you are writing on, that's the main thing. In fact it's the *only* thing!

82. **Make health a part of your wealth** and look after it like the precious jewel that it is. If you don't look after your physical body, who do you think will? Right now, see if you can think of any areas where you are not honouring yourself, and promise yourself you are going to do something about it.

83. **Make a decision to be a role model** to others in your life when it comes to following your dreams and making yourself a success. Show don't tell.

Don't talk about it, do it!

84. **Inspire yourself by reading business books and autobiographies.** I also love to create my own inspiration books by finding inspiring articles of someone I admire online, and copying and pasting them into a Word document to read later.

85. **Learn to deeply and completely love and accept yourself** exactly as you are. This is huge, and still something I can struggle with. I like to cultivate new thought patterns to help with this, such as, 'There is no hurry', 'You are okay exactly where you are', and the ever-soothing 'All is well'.

86. **Declutter your workspace** (and your home) often, keeping it as a creative, sacred and motivating place to inspire, refresh and connect you.

87. **Have an ideas document** on your computer where you note down *everything*: Brainwaves for your writing, words that you adore which could form the basis of a piece, requests from readers, favourite quotes, a blog subject idea you've seen somewhere else and loved e.g. '7 things you don't know about me', and anything else that sparks your imagination.

88. **Become someone who is a completer of tasks.** This has changed everything for me. When

I focus on tying up loose ends and completing projects, it creates a feelgood flow-on effect. Having messy piles and half-done projects hanging around is a major energy drain.

89. **Switch your computer off when you are not working**, otherwise you could be drawn back to the screen and end up doodling your time away. It's important to spend time in real life either with yourself or your loved ones. Not only is it more balanced, but you will find greater inspiration than being at a screen all the time.

90. **Commit to following your dream** of becoming a published author and do whatever it takes to get there! Disregard naysayers, procrastination, your own self-limiting beliefs, doubts, fear, worry, perceived lack of time, not being good enough and all those BS 'reasons' why you shouldn't be successful.

91. **Capture ideas as you receive them.** Jot a note down. Speak the idea into the voice recorder on your phone. Write an email to yourself. I have found that even waiting a few minutes can cause the exact formation of words to be lost forever.

92. **Set yourself goals that motivate you**, whether it's word count goals, task goals or time-spent-typing goals. I like to mix it up. Different goals

inspire me to kick butt at different times. What never grows old though is the feeling of checking off that achievement, even if small.

93. **Speak positively about everything in your life** as much as possible, especially your writing. Train yourself to be one of those people who always sees the good in any given situation, person or event. There are two sides to a coin, and one is always in the shadow. Choose the brightly lit side of the coin as much as possible.

94. **Find out what your beliefs on being successful, prosperous, and driven are** – write them down and ask yourself if they are true. If they are good ones, keep them and be thankful for them. If they are not, declutter them.

95. **To find inspiration** for new blog posts or anything else you wish to write, look back at your previous work and inspire fresh ideas that way.

96. **Consider the source.** If you are offered 'helpful' advice by someone, ask yourself, 'Is the person offering this advice a successful published author who is going places?' It's highly likely they are not, which means you can thank them for their concern and go on quite happily ignoring their advice.

97. **You are who you are.** Learn to love yourself. That's all :)

98. **Your voice can make a difference.** A similar message or even the same message might have been said by someone else, but you are coming in fresh with a completely different viewpoint – *your* viewpoint. No-one else can write the book you write!

99. **Celebrate every little achievement:** When you publish a blog post. When you finish a chapter. When you receive your first fan email. When you do what you told yourself you were going to do that day. Give yourself a verbal high-five and enjoy the satisfying feeling of achievement.

100. **And finally, be thankful** you are the age you are in the time you are living in right now – you are exactly where you are meant to be and it is your time to be prosperous and fabulous, right now – enjoy it!

That's it, my chic author friends. I hope you are inspired and motivated by this book. Perhaps there is one point that jumps out at you right now? Why not activate something new and create ripples in your own universe?

'Do it now' is one of my favourite mantras and I leave it with you. *Do it now.*

A Note from the Author

It was such a pleasure to write this book and I truly hope you have enjoyed reading it. I would be thrilled to think that in some small way I have inspired you to consider your own life differently; to live beautifully and well, to embrace your eccentricities and know that what you love is entirely okay.

When you have a moment, I would be so grateful if you could write an honest review on Amazon. These reviews are vital to authors and will help other chic ladies like yourself find my books.

Whether you have read all my books, or this is your first one, I thank you for being here. If you want to write, you can contact me at: fiona@howtobechic.com. I'd love to hear what chapter you enjoyed most and ideas you have put into practice.

With all my love,

About the Author

Fiona Ferris is passionate about, and has studied the topic of living well for more than twenty years, in particular that a simple and beautiful life can be achieved without spending a lot of money.

Fiona finds inspiration from all over the place including Paris and France, the countryside, big cities, fancy hotels, music, beautiful scents, magazines, books, all those fabulous blogs out there, people, pets, nature, other countries and cultures; really, everywhere she looks.

Fiona lives in the beautiful and sunny wine region of Hawke's Bay, New Zealand, with her husband, Paul, their rescue cats Jessica and Nina and rescue dogs Daphne and Chloe.

To learn more about Fiona, you can connect with her at:

howtobechic.com
fionaferris.com
facebook.com/fionaferrisauthor
twitter.com/fiona_ferris
instagram.com/fionaferrisnz
youtube.com/fionaferris

Book Bonuses

http://bit.ly/ThirtyChicDaysBookBonuses

Type in the link above to receive your free special bonuses.

'21 ways to be chic' is a fun list of chic living reminders, with an MP3 recording to accompany it so you can listen on the go as well.

Excerpts from all of Fiona's books in PDF format.

You will also **receive a subscription** to Fiona's blog *'How to be Chic'*, for regular inspiration on living a simple, beautiful and successful life.

Printed in Great Britain
by Amazon